FROM THE DUNGHILL TO THE THRONE

Nathaniel Saingbe

FROM THE DUNGHILL TO THE THRONE

Copyright © 2021 by

Nathaniel Kogi Saingbe
NAKS Publications
Nakspublications@gmail.com

Paperback ISBN: 978-1-952098-54-3
eBook ISBN: 978-1-952098-55-0

Printed in the United States of America. All rights reserved solely by the author. No part of this publication may be reproduced in any form, stored in a retrieval system, or transmitted in any form by any means - electronic, mechanical, photocopy except with the written permission of the Author. Unless otherwise noted, Bible quotations are taken from the Holy Bible, New King James Version (NKJV) Copyright 1982 by Thomas Nelson, Inc., publishers. Used by permission.

Published by Cornerstone Publishing
A Division of Cornerstone Creativity Group LLC
www.thecornerstonepublishers.com

DEDICATION

To the love of my life, Jumoke. Destiny brought us together many years ago; and to our beloved children, Ritozeh and Rikeh. With you by my side, the intricacies of ministerial work have always been made easy. We shall together finish well in Jesus's name!

ACKNOWLEDGMENTS

My depth of appreciation goes to the Lord God Almighty under whose protective arms I have come this far. You picked me from the dunghill and have caused me to be among the living. My journey to the throne is within sight, and I do not doubt that Your able hands will propel me to the glorious top.

I appreciate my wonderful parents, who invested in me and brought me up in fear of the Lord. Thank you, Dad, for your passionate prayer always; and to my mom of blessed memory.

How can I forget you, Dominion Chapel Family; Your prayers and support have kept my family and I going over the years. Together, we have overcome obstacles and risen above challenges. The best is yet to come!

I acknowledge my friend and colleague in the ministry whose immense contribution has made this see the limelight. The Lord bless you and meet you at the point of your needs.

My editors and the entire Cornerstone Publishing team, you are highly appreciated.

CONTENTS

Dedication..3
Acknowledgments..4
Introduction...7
1. You Are Not An Accident......................................9
2. Greatness Knows No Birthplace...........................17
3. Configured For Greatness....................................27
4. Possibilities Of God's In You...............................33
5. Necessity Of Divine Connection..........................43
6. Stay Connected To Your Source..........................51
7. Key Steps To Reaching The Throne.....................59
8. Conquering Obstacles To The Throne.................73
9. See It, Have It..87
10. Vision Provides Direction....................................95
11. The Mentality Of Kings.....................................103
12. Reigning Like Royalty.......................................113
References..119

INTRODUCTION

Whenever we think of a throne, the first thing that readily comes to mind is royalty and succession. This perception, however, can make us think that the throne only belongs to a few lucky people. This is why the minds of many people find it difficult to process how an individual can move from the dunghill to the throne. *How can a beggar become a king? How can someone with a poor background rise to become a global celebrity?* In short, how can someone seemingly destined for failure defy all odds to become a success?

Our minds can deceive us into thinking that kings and champions are born and cannot be made. Yet, studies have proved over and over again that, with the right attitude, anyone can do extraordinary things. Affirming this, a Professor of Psychology once stated that people who achieve the seemingly impossible are not necessarily extraordinary people. Rather, they are people who struggle extremely hard and persist in pursing their vision of greatness. They enjoy their work. They excel at concentrating and persevering. Their effort is focused, and they have a firm sense of direction. This underscores the fact that there is no such thing as an overnight success; getting to the throne requires a lot of grit, focus, and diligence.

This book has been written especially for you to know that you also can be on the throne because that is God's desire for you. You can be celebrated as a problem-solver and solution-provider. Here, you will discover that your biggest dreams can come true and that your background does not have to determine your access to the throne.

Many people are languishing at the dunghill because they are either ignorant of some salient principles, or they have refused to act wisely. Ben Carson did not start out as the best among the rest. In fact, he was at rock bottom as a child in elementary school. However, the moment he began to activate the success principles his mom taught him, he began to rise till he became the first successful black neurosurgeon in the world. His decision to be diligent and disciplined got him to the throne.

God's desire is for you is to be successful and He longs for you to reign, as a King's child truly should. This book will show you how to bring this desire to manifestation in your life. Yes, you can rise from "nothingness" to prominence. Enough of playing on small fields, it is time for you to move to the big league!

1

YOU ARE NOT AN ACCIDENT

"You can judge the value and worth of a product by looking at the one who made it. You are no accident. You were created by God, for God."
- Mary Southerland

One of the most inspiring stories that demonstrate the wonders of divine grace in human destiny is that of King David in the Bible. He was the last child of his father; yet the Bible reveals that he was usually sent to the wilderness to shepherd his father's flock. Can you imagine that? How do you send your last child on such a dangerous adventure when he has seven older ones? Well, the answer seems pretty obvious. David was the least recognized and least cherished in his family; nobody ever thought he could amount to anything in life or even do something great.

In fact, a historian painted this touching picture of how pitiable David's early life was: "David was not permitted to eat with the rest of his family, but was assigned to a separate table in the corner. He was given the task of a shepherd because 'they hoped that a wild beast would come and kill him while he was performing his duties,' and for this reason was sent to pasture in dangerous areas full of lions and bears."

But something happened that completely changed the narrative for David. One day, he was taking care of the sheep somewhere in the wilderness when Prophet Samuel visited his father's house to select a king for the nation of Israel. 1 Samuel 16:1 says:

> "Now the Lord said to Samuel, "How long will you mourn for Saul, seeing I have rejected him from reigning over Israel? Fill your horn with oil, and go; I am sending you to Jesse the Bethlehemite. For I have provided Myself a king among his sons"

When Samuel got to Bethlehem, Jesse's sons were lined up before him, and the selection for the person to succeed King Saul began. Samuel examined the seven sons of Jesse that were before him and would have settled for one of them if God had not stopped him. God told him none of the seven sons before him qualified to be king. There was one more person Samuel had not seen: David. Yes, he was the least expected. They had even forgotten that David was also a son of Jesse until Samuel inquired if there was anyone else. Yes, came the answer, but he was far away in the bush!

Samuel insisted he must be fetched. In fact, they all would not sit until he came. Jesse sent for David. David appeared in his shepherd's garment, exhausted from the day's work. God spoke to Samuel that David was the person He had chosen to be the next king of Israel, and Samuel anointed him immediately.

> *"And Samuel said to Jesse, "Send and bring him. For we will not sit down till he comes here." So he sent and brought him in. Now he was ruddy, with bright eyes, and good-looking. And the Lord said, "Arise, anoint him; for this is the one!" Then Samuel took the horn of oil and anointed him in the midst of his brothers; and the Spirit of the Lord came upon David from that day forward. So Samuel arose and went to Ramah" (1 Samuel 16:11-14).*

David was the forgotten one. He was the child with the least expectations, and the child everyone thought was not good enough for anything except to take care of animals. He was only remembered when the prophet prodded his father. However, despite being in the background and almost forgotten, and even though his parents apparently had no plan for his future, God sent Samuel to specifically anoint him to be king over Israel.

God's Special Plan

You can see the sovereignty of God's providence here. God was intentional about David. Prophet Samuel anointing him as king shows that God knew him before he was born and had a plan for him; he was not an accident. By divine orchestration, David went from the son who was forgotten in obscurity to the anointed king over God's chosen people—he went from the dunghill to the throne because God had a plan for his life.

A lot of people go through life like they are a mistake of nature. Because of certain conditions surrounding their lives, they feel they are that child who was not planned for but stubbornly came into the world. If you are one of such persons, I am here to tell you that in that family you have found yourself, you are not a mistake and God has a plan for you.

Perhaps, your parents have told you stories about how they had put an end to childbirth, but you defied all that they had done and still came. Perhaps, they remind you of how you were the unexpected child who changed their plans, and these statements make you feel like you are unwanted. They make you feel you are just a mistake that should never have happened. I want you to know that even though your parent might not have had plans for you, to God, you are not an accident; He was very intentional about creating you and allowing you to come into this world and even into your particular family.

There is the story of a woman who happened to be the last born of the family—the unexpected, stubborn one who forced herself in. This was the narrative she grew up with, coupled with the fact that she did not "bring wealth" from heaven, as it is believed that some children do when they are born like that. Because of the humble background she had, she suffered a lot - from hawking fruits on the streets of Ibadan (a city in southwestern Nigeria) to doing menial jobs. But along the line, she began to see herself differently from what people called her. She began to believe deeply within herself that God had plans for her. By divine providence, she migrated to a commonwealth country and began to climb the ladder of her career until she got to the top. In a recent ceremony by the government of Canada, she was awarded as part of the top twenty-five successful immigrants in Canada.

Let this story and many others that you may have heard serve as an encouragement to you, if you believe you are that child who is not needed. Do not let your background put your back to the ground, or make you think God just dumped you on this earth to suffer, or that you were an afterthought or a mistake. You are not any of these!

You are a Masterpiece

Now, let us explore God's mind, purpose, and plan for your life. The Bible reveals clearly that God has good and peaceful thoughts toward you, and He intends to give you a hope and a future (Jeremiah 29:11). This passage should give you an understanding of the privilege you have as God's creation. If you were an afterthought, God would not have bothered designing a special plan for your life. But because you are not an accident, He has plans for you, plans of peace and not of evil.

Let me show you two passages of the Scripture that prove that you were intentionally made and masterfully crafted before you were placed on this earth to fulfil a definite purpose. Isaiah 44:2 says, "*Thus says the Lord who made you And formed you from the womb, who will help you...*" And in Jeremiah 1:5, God clearly reveals, "*Before I formed you in the womb I knew you; Before you were born I sanctified you...*".

Both of these passages clearly tells you that you were not an afterthought. If God could boldly and clearly say that He FORMED you; and that before you were formed, He had known you, it shows the depth of His plans for you. Though God may not have called you to be a prophet like He said to Jeremiah, I want you to know that He has called you for a specific purpose and has designed you with all the things that you need to achieve the purpose for which He has created you.

You are God's masterpiece! God never makes an accidental work or a work of mistake; He is intentional and purposeful. He created you with the end in mind—He knew everything you would become and achieve in life, and He created in you everything you would need to get there. So, dear friend, stop seeing yourself as a mistake or an unfortunate child or anything else—you are wonderfully and fearfully made (Psalm 139:14) by the Almighty God!

Considering the intentionality with which you were made, you should be convinced by now that you are unique - with unique abilities, characteristics, and intelligence. So, next time that thought of you being an accident crosses your mind, remind yourself of what God says: "You're fearfully and wonderfully made."

2

GREATNESS KNOWS NO BIRTHPLACE

"To be a star, you must shine your own light, follow your own path, and don't worry about darkness, for that is when the stars shine brightest"
- Napoleon Hill

Where you were born has nothing to do with where God is taking you to. It is true that you had no say as to which family you were born in, and where you were born. But God, being the master planner had a purpose for the decision He made for you. He is the ultimate decider, and because He is the One who has your destiny in His hands, you can be sure that it will definitely be well with you.

So, it does not matter what part of the world you are

now, or the place of your birth or where you have been. Whatever situation or family you were born into — it is not your fault. It is what you will do from now on that will determine how far you will go!

Jephthah in the Bible is a perfect example of someone who did not let the circumstances of his birth determine his altitude. You will find his story in Judges 11. The first thing you notice as you read his story is that his mother was a prostitute. That should ordinarily have knocked him out of the race to prominence in life, as he was considered an illegitimate child. Like Joseph, he was hated by his brothers and thrown out, denying him of a share of their father's inheritance. But because Jephthah's life had a purpose and he had been born into the house of Gilead at the right time, his brothers had no choice but to seek him to save them from the war the children of Ammon waged against the children of Israel.

Thus, from being the despised son of a harlot, Jephthah became the leader of Israel. Now, do you see that no one ever comes into the world by mistake? There is no such thing as mistake in God's book. You were intentionally placed in the house you were born into.

Born to Be a Game-Changer

We could say that Joseph was born into bitter rivalry, considering the situation in his family as at the time of his birth. He also became the favorite child of his father, which further aggravated the jealousy and hatred of his brothers. The day that seemed to be the beginning of his end was when his father sent him to the field to check out his brothers. They had sighted him afar off and plotted amongst themselves to send him to an early grave, but he was divinely saved by the advice of one of them. Eventually, he was sold off to some slave buyers.

Joseph ended up in Potiphar's house in Egypt as a slave boy. It looked as though life was against him, and everywhere he turned seemed to be a point of trouble for him. His rejection of the advances of his master's wife led him to the prison. He spent some years in prison, and really, it would have seemed that he had been forgotten or that God was unaware of his plight. Right? Not at all. After years of being forgotten, God's plan for Joseph was fulfilled. If he had not gone through the path he went, he might not have fulfilled his purpose. God lifted him out of the dungeon and set him in the palace to be in charge of the kingdom as next in command after Pharaoh. Someone who came from a rough background and went through a turbulent path was lifted from the dunghill and exalted.

The Omnipotent Lifter

Joseph's story should be a pointer to the fact that even if you seem to be in the dunghill of life, God can lift you out of it. The Bible says that God *"raiseth up the poor out of the dust, and lifteth up the beggar from the dunghill, to set them among princes, and to make them inherit the throne of glory* " (1 Samuel 2:8, KJV). Did you notice that it does not just say that God raises the poor and beggar to inherit "the throne", but to inherit "the throne of glory"? Is not this awesome!

I need you to also understand that a dunghill is not just a heap of dung, but "a repugnant, filthy, or degraded place." Imagine someone who is in a situation that is so repugnant, filthy, and degraded. You will agree that it is only the omnipotent God who can bring such a person out. The way God took Joseph out of that hopeless situation, having been locked up in what we could call a maximum-security prison, and set him up in the palace of Pharaoh, is the same way God will take you out of whatever limitation or situation you may have found yourself in.

Let me remind you again that there is nothing that happens to you that is beyond God's knowledge. He created you for a purpose, and He has the script of your life in His palm. He is ever mindful of all that concerns your life. He says in Isaiah 49:15-16, "*Can a woman forget her nursing child, And not have compassion on the son of her womb? Surely they may forget, Yet I will not forget you. See, I have inscribed you on the palms of My hands; Your walls are continually before Me.*"

The Word of God further affirms that God takes you,

cleanses you, beautifies you, promotes you, elevates you, makes ways for you, and moves on your behalf until you inherit the throne of glory! I want you to know that when God is ready to lift you, nothing else matters—not where you were born, not your language, not your location. Nothing else!

Celebrate Your Uniqueness

"Celebrate your uniqueness!" This was the declaration from the man of God that renewed the spirit of Judith, as she strategically positioned herself on the first row at the center of the auditorium directly facing the pulpit. She had often wondered what positive contributions could be made in her generation by a person with a "unique but weird" nature like her.

Born as the only crippled and visually impaired child of her parents, reflections about her conception being a mistake constantly flowed through her mind. But on that fateful day —December 25, 2012 – something dramatic happened to her. She stopped seeing herself as a girl born by accident and started seeing herself as one who was created and placed in this generation at such a time as this to show forth the praise of Him that thought it good for her to be so wonderfully and fearfully made.

Judith's story is similar to the experience of many people. Not all might be physically handicapped as Judith was, but a majority still allow themselves to be entrapped and sucked up by the mentality that their coming to this world was by chance and with no divinely ordained purpose to fulfill.

So, you see, your existence in whatever part of the world, through whatever family history you came from, was all intentional and just what God needed to make you a wonder unto many. There is a purpose and role you have to play on earth, which no one else can fulfill. Isn't that enough reason for you to see yourself as a unique blessing to your family, church, society, generation, and the world at large?

Manger-Born Messiah

Where you were born, your language, or your race cannot hinder you from becoming what you were born to be, except you allow it. I cannot emphasize this enough. Take another look at the birth of Jesus CHRIST, our Lord, and you will see the truth of this fact revealed there. In Luke 2:7, the Bible says that Mary " *brought forth her firstborn Son, and wrapped Him in swaddling cloths, and laid Him in a manger, because there was no room for them in the inn.*"

Swaddling clothes are ordinary clothes used to wrap babies to keep them warm; there is nothing exotic or special about them. Note also that the Messiah was born in a manger! Can you believe that? Jesus, who was destined to be the Savior of the whole world, was born in a stable where cattle or horses feed. He did not even have the luxury of being born into a well-built and tastefully furnished inn, not to talk of a world-class hospital! Christ's background and place of birth was indeed a humbling one for the kind of assignment He was sent to fulfill, but did that alter His dream? Did it stop Him from fulfilling His destiny? Did it make any difference in who He became? NO!

You pity yourself and say,

> *"If only I was born into a certain family; if only I was of the other race; if only I was born better - you know, more handsome or beautiful than the way I look now, perhaps things would be different."*

Let me tell you this: all of these have nothing to do with where God is taking you to.

Where Jesus was born did not make Him less capable of fulfilling His destiny. In fact, His lowly background should settle it in your mind that greatness knows no birthplace. God has designed everything about your life to work together to fulfill His greater purposes for you. What could be more delightful!

Again, see the Psalmist's confession in Psalm 139: 14-17:

> *" I will praise You, for I am fearfully and wonderfully made; Marvelous are Your works, And that my soul knows very well. My frame was not hidden from You, When I was made in secret, And skillfully wrought in the lowest parts of the earth. Your eyes saw my substance,*

being yet unformed. And in Your book they all were written, The days fashioned for me, When as yet there were none of them. How precious also are Your thoughts to me, O God! How great is the sum of them!".

This is one of the psalms of David that buttress the fact that everything about you was perfectly outlined. You are an intricate design masterfully crafted by the all-knowing God — no detail about you was left out.

Your Ultimate Destination

The way you look has nothing to do with your destiny and where God is taking you to. That you were born without a silver spoon does not mean you will not be able to sit on tables laid with gold. What you are experiencing now is not an indication of who you will be in the future. God is in the business of giving pleasant surprises. People may be looking down on you now; they may consider you to be a never-do-well in life because of your current state. Your parents, siblings or friends may have written you off and considered you a lost cause, but I want to assure you that God is yet to start with you.

Here is the inspiring story of Alexander Hamilton, the United States' first secretary of treasury, as told by Evans Andrews. Alexander was the illegitimate son of a Scottish father and a French Huguenot mother who was still married to another man. His father abandoned the family when he was 10, and his mother died a few years later from fever. In 1773, a group of local businessmen raised money to send him to school in New York. He delved into politics and served as the aide-de-camp to General George Washington during the American Revolution. Alexander who was once called "the bastard brat of a Scottish peddler" became someone who played a pivotal role in shaping the American political system.

I do not know what your situation is, but you can rest assured that your days of small beginnings are over, and God is taking you to the top. Remember, your background does not determine where you are going, and you are by no chance an accident. You were in God's plan from the get-go!

3

CONFIGURED FOR GREATNESS

"The gift of sonship to God become ours not through being born, but through being born again."

- J.I. Packer

I am not a scientist, neither am I a medical doctor to authoritatively speak on the origin of the DNA (Deoxyribonucleic Acid); but suffice to say that DNA is a unique replicating material present in ALL organisms. It is a molecule that contains the biological instructions that make each species unique. DNA, along with the instructions it contains, is passed from adult organisms to their offspring during reproduction. Basically, what it does is that it carries and transfers genetic information from one organism to the other. Sometimes, it carries it from generation to generation.

This explains why the ancestry of a person can easily be deduced when a DNA test is conducted on them. Not only that, but it is also scientifically possible to determine the percentage of DNA a child got from the father or the mother. The reason is that there is a transfer of characteristics from the parent to the child.

Dear reader, I can tell you that as one of God's special creations, there is a transfer of the power of God, the victory of God, and the excellence of God to you. You have the DNA of God in you! By virtue of your creation, you carry some attributes of God in you. You carry divinity inside of you. And if your gene is made up of divine composites, then you can never be anything short of who God is.

Let me show you a proof of what I have just stated. In Genesis 1:26-31, the Scripture narrates:

> *"Then God said, "Let Us make man in Our image, according to Our likeness; let them have dominion over the fish of the sea, over the birds of the air, and over the cattle, over all the earth and over every creeping thing that creeps on the earth." So God created man in His own image; in the image of God He created him; male and female He created them. Then God blessed them, and God said to them, "Be fruitful and multiply; fill the earth and subdue it; have dominion over the fish of the sea, over the birds of the air, and over every living thing that moves on the earth... Then God saw everything that*

He had made, and indeed it was VERY GOOD. So the evening and the morning were the sixth day."

Quite interesting, isn't it? God saw that everything He created was very good – and that includes you. Perhaps you are in the habit of looking down on yourself. You constantly compare your physical features to those of your siblings, friends, neighbors, and others, and have thereby developed an inferiority complex. Whenever you stand before the mirror, you pity yourself! You do not consider yourself beautiful enough or smart enough or able to get certain things done. Please, get this again. The Almighty God who created you said He created you to be "very good" and not just "good'.!

Affirmation of Your Divine DNA

Now, you may want to ask, what are the proofs that I have the DNA of God? Here are the answers: One, you were created and formed in God's image and likeness; and two, when He created you, He breathed the breath of life into you. If you look at Genesis 2:7, the Bible says, *"And the Lord God formed man of the dust of the ground, and breathed into his nostrils the breath of life; and man became a living being."*

We see here that after God had created Adam, the progenitor of all humans, from the dust in His likeness and image, He breathed into his nostril *the breath of life.*

Not only did He breathe into him, but the first word God spoke to him was also a BLESSING! God said to Him, "You are blessed!" And God gave him authority and began to prophesy into the life that He had just created. You have the breath of God in you – this is one reason you should not fail.

However, there is an even more powerful way that God has breathed into you, and that is through the work of your redemption if you have been born again. By that special work of grace, you have been redeemed from the Adamic nature—the one that the enemy corrupted. Jesus came, and redeemed us by His blood! As many as believe in that atoning blood, to them, He gives the power to become the children of God (John 1:12). Today, those of us who are born again (children of God) have access to yet another BREATH, which is the breath of the Holy Spirit. The Holy Spirit is God in us, teaching and directing us.

Essentially, you have the DNA of God because the Word of God says so! In fact, as you look into the Scripture, you will discover that even Jesus confirmed that we are "gods". But before we get to that, Genesis 1:27 from the Message Bible reads, *"God created human beings; he created them godlike, reflecting God's nature. He created them male and female."* This essentially means that you are a GODLIKE being. You look like God; you have the image of God and you have the breath of God in you.

Now, here is that powerful declaration from Christ in John 10:34-35. *"Jesus answered them, "Is it not written in your law, 'I said, "You are gods"'? If He called them gods, to whom the word of God came (and the Scripture cannot be broken)."* When God created you, He put His DNA in you. He put His gene in you; you look like your Father. A lion cannot give birth to a cat. It can never happen. In the same manner, you cannot be different from your heavenly Father. You cannot possess an attribute that your father does not possess. If he cannot fail, then, know for sure that you can never fail! Hallelujah!

So many times, you see a couple giving birth to a spitting image of themselves in their children. You see that a child can either look, act, and behave like either of the parents. Why is this so? You will realize that genetic power is at work, which is a function of the DNA. In the same way, having God's DNA means partaking in the nature of God. It means you have been configured to live the life of power, authority, dominion, excellence, and prosperity – just as your Father!

4

POSSIBILITIES OF GOD'S DNA IN YOU

"Those that be planted in the house of the LORD shall flourish in the courts of our God."
- Psalm 92:12

Having established that you have the DNA of God, you need to know the dimensions of operations of this supernatural component of your being. What is the essence? What should be the result of your being formed in the likeness of the Almighty God?

One, **the DNA of God in you is for prosperity.** It is written in the scriptures, *"The earth is the Lord's, and all its fullness"* (Psalm 24:1). Your Father owns all the wealth in this world and he sure delights in your prosperity. Have you seen very wealthy parents whose children live in penury? Of course not. That will be an anomaly.

If you read Psalm 92:12-14, the word of God says, "*The righteous shall flourish like a palm tree, He shall grow like a cedar in Lebanon. Those who are planted in the house of the Lord Shall flourish in the courts of our God. They shall still bear fruit in old age;* ***They shall be fresh and flourishing.***" You see - the Word of God says you will look fresh; it says you will flourish.

You will not prosper if you do not believe that it is God's will for you to prosper. It is clearly written in Deuteronomy 8:18, "*And you shall remember the Lord your God, for it is He who gives you the power to get wealth, that He may establish His covenant Which He swore to your fathers, as it is this day.*" When we talk about prosperity, it does not have to do with financial prosperity alone. It cuts across every area of your life, including your marriage, career, ministry, and life endeavors.

However, your financial prosperity is dependent on your obedience to God's word and principle on financial prosperity. You can see this in Luke 6:38 which says, "*give, and it shall be given to you: good measure, pressed down, shaken together, and running over will be put into your bosom. For with the same measure that you use, it will be measured back to you.*"

Secondly, **the DNA of God in you is for you to reproduce.**

When God was charging up Adam with the authority that comes from being His first creation, He said, *"Be fruitful and multiply"* (Genesis 1:28). The emphasis here, is on the word, "multiply". The capacity to take one thing and turn it into yet another thing is ours to inherit in God. We have the capacity to nurture and bring a concept or human to life.

Our father does not take delight in the death but exponential increase of whatever He has entrusted into our hands. We see this play out in the parable Jesus told of a certain master and his servants in Matthew 25:14-30. This master, while embarking on a journey, gave each of his servants five, two and one talent, respectively. The Scripture explains what happened thereafter this way, *"Then he who had received the five talents went and traded with them, and made another five talents."* You see reproduction playing out there, right? The Bible goes further to explain, *"And likewise he who had received two gained two more also. But he who had received one went and dug in the ground, and hid his lord's money."*

The conclusion of the parable is that the ones who utilized what they had and reproduced received a commendation from their lord while the one who hid his received a rebuke and was severely punished.

The above story clearly reveals that the Lord expects us to nurture every single gift or talent He has committed into our hands to the point of multiplication. You have the capacity to bring to life. You have the capacity to bring that business idea to life and in turn, make it a big venture. You have the capacity to birth sons and daughters, spiritually and biologically. This capacity comes through the gene of the Almighty in you. And you do know that that gene is one of reproduction. No one can explain the mystery of conception down to delivery; this is one of the mighty miracles of God.

I pray for you this day that you will not be barren. Please understand that barrenness is not peculiar to childbearing. It has to do with the entirety of your life down to what you do! Again, I prophesy that you will continually increase in life.

Thirdly, **the DNA of God in you is for dominance**. With the DNA of God comes the capacity to dominate and rule your world! To dominate means to have control over someone or something. It means to be in charge. Dominance, in the light of the Word of God, does not mean you oppress people because of your position. That is the way of the world and we are not of the world.

I love how Dr. Nick Van puts it in an article he wrote a few years ago. He said, *"God did not make us to be passive and to float down the river like a dead fish, he gave us strength, power, authority and ability to subdue, dominate and overpower unscriptural circumstances. Don't just sit there and sing, "que sera, sera, whatever will be, will be, the future's not ours to see, que sera, sera."* Assess your life, measure it up against the word, and then access grace and use every ounce of the ability of Jesus in you, every ounce of your supernatural authority, strength, and innovativeness in Christ, and take charge!

I know this is a strong expression, but if you do not take charge and exercise real dominion and authority over the circumstances of your life, the devil, people, and situations will dominate you and steal everything that God has given you! The Word of God says, you *"will be the head and not the tail"* (Deuteronomy 28:13). Do you know that some people have erroneously believed that it is their job to rule over you and it is yours to obey? Hard to hear, but it is the reality. Sadly, a lot of persons have accepted that reality.

God was not mincing words when He said you will be the head and not the tail. You have to let that sink into your subconscious, so that you do not become relegated to the position of the tail where you don't belong. Really, in life, what you tolerate is what becomes your reality. So many persons tolerate strife, lack, depression, fear, sickness, and other negative circumstances. They allow the devil to come in and steal, and then they go on to accuse God of forsaking them. The earlier you come to realize that our heavenly Father controls the universe and, what more, we are His children and have been given dominion and authority to rule and reign in His name, the better things will begin to align for your good.

I encourage you to take charge! You have divinity flowing through your veins. You cannot cower before the forces of darkness. You are in charge through the power of Christ in you. I make a decree that you will get to the top because that is where you are meant to be.

Four, **the DNA of God in you is for enlargement.** To enlarge means to make broad and large beyond what exists. Jabez was an individual who understood the power of praying for the enlargement of his coast. This was someone that was restricted on every side and wanted a change to that situation. He called for divine intervention, and God transformed his destiny. The gene of God that you carry does not permit playing small. It does not permit mediocrity. It does not permit limitations. Therefore, if you see traces of limitations and restrictions in your life, cry out like Jabez did and exercise your authority in GOD.

The Word of God says you will not be few; you will not be small. You will have an abundance of whatsoever your hands finds to do. I pray to the Lord to make you a thousand times more than you are right now!

Five, **the DNA of God in you is for control.** The story is told of a young man who struggled with masturbation. The struggle went on for about five years and each time he indulged in that sinful act, he hated himself for it. Years down the line, he surrendered his life to Jesus and fought that monster of masturbation through the word of

God. He constantly affirmed his victory in Christ Jesus and at the same time, blocked access to all channels of temptation. He realized the authority he had in Jesus and used that to confront the enemy of his soul. Months after, he discovered that it had been a while he masturbated or watched pornographic materials. That was the moment of his victory.

The word of God says in Genesis 1:26-31,

> *"Then God said, "Let Us make man in Our image, according to Our likeness; let them have dominion over the fish of the sea, over the birds of the air, and over the cattle, over all the earth and over every creeping thing that creeps on the earth." So God created man in His own image; in the image of God He created him; male and female He created them. Then God blessed them, and God said to them, "Be fruitful and multiply; fill the earth and subdue it; have dominion over the fish of the sea, over the birds of the air, and over every living thing that moves on the earth."... Then God saw everything that He had made, and indeed it was very good. So the evening and the morning were the sixth day.."*

For you to subdue, you should be able to be in control. You can control what you do, control the situation and circumstances that you do not agree with on your knees. You can control them!

What are the things you have control over? One, the evil powers that seek to control your life and family. You can command them to leave because you have the right, the power, and the authority. Two, sicknesses, diseases, oppressions, afflictions and all the powers of the enemy. You have control over all of these, and nothing shall by any means hurt you (Luke 10;19).

I mentioned it earlier that when the first humans – Adam and Eve – were created, "God blessed them." What does that mean? He commanded them to prosper, to reproduce, and to fill the earth! In other words, God has given you the audacity, the authority, the right for you to prosper, the right for you to reproduce, fill the earth, take charge and be responsible. I pray for you that whatever has been holding you back from prospering, reproducing, filling the earth, and taking charge will be removed by the power of the Almighty God. The Lord will move you higher. You will expand and enlarge beyond your limitations. The heavens will be open unto you and you will enter into your divine destiny.

Isaiah 51:1-2 says,

> *"Listen to me, you who follow after righteousness. You who seek the Lord: look to the rock from which you were hewn. And to the hole of the pit from which you were dug. Look to Abraham your father, and to Sarah who bore you; For I called him alone, And BLESSED him and INCREASED him."*

This is the God that we serve! I want you to know that as a child of God, God is not yet done with you. Your best is yet to come. And you know what? The best wine, like in the story of the wedding in Cana of Galilee, was reserved for the last moment! Those who are mocking you, thinking you cannot amount to anything significant in life, have not seen anything yet. You know why? Because God is taking you somewhere.

It is impossible for you not to make it with all of God's deposits in you. You will definitely succeed. Whatever may be the mountain, valley, or impossibility standing in your way, I say unto you that because you have the DNA of God in you, you will cross over. Isaiah 3:10 says, *"Say to the righteous that it shall be well with them, for they shall eat the fruit of their doings"*

In Psalm 8:4-6, the word of God says God has crowned humans with glory and honor. He has given us dominion over the works of His hands. He has put all things on the earth under our feet. What glorious revelation! Do you know God has put all things under your feet? Whether they are demons, principalities, sicknesses, diseases, infirmities, whatever that is! And the Bible says that every weapon that comes against you shall not prosper. Are you facing an obstacle? God has put all things under your control. I pray that you will come to terms with your true identity in God!

Again, get this: a lion cannot give birth to a cat. You cannot be different from your heavenly Father. Whatever you do, have that at the back of your mind. You are royalty! You are a child of the Almighty! You rule and you dominate!

5

NECESSITY OF DIVINE CONNECTION

"There are two kinds of people: those who say to God, 'Thy will be done,' and those to whom God says, 'All right, then, have it your way'".

— *C. S. Lewis*

Before we proceed further, let me ask you some vital questions: "Who is riding with you in your life's journey? Who is leading you, in your journey to the throne? Where are you getting your instructions from? `

If you want to make a successful journey from the dunghill to the throne, you need God to be by your side. Or better put, you need to be on God's side. You cannot leave God out and do your own things, and then expect to succeed!

It is a terrible mistake to leave God out of the equation. Sadly, many people discovered this too late in their journey.

Many have questioned the relevance of God in our daily living. But having established the fact that we have the DNA of God, you should know that you cannot do things outside His gene. You cannot afford to live by chance. You do not even have to live by chance. Your Father is an all-powerful God who controls the universe and has your life planned out. Would you, therefore, live life by chance when you can easily consult the One that made that life?

The "God Factor" in Your Success

Do you need God? Oh yes, you do! You do need the One who breathed the breath of life into you. You need the One whom everything in this life and beyond exists in. You need the One who parted the Red Sea. You need the one that took an insignificant shepherd boy and made him king. You need the One who took the rejected dreamer and crowned him prime minister in a foreign land. You need the One who changed the history of a man whose name depicts sorrow and hardship, and brought him to the limelight. Dear reader, you need God!

Why do you need God on your way to the throne? Because He is the Beginning and the End, the Alpha, and the Omega. He alone has the power to accomplish all that has been written concerning you from the foundations of the world. From 1 Samuel 2:7-8, we already know that promotion comes from God; nobody can become anything unless God makes them so. The Scripture says the Lord makes both the poor and the rich; He brings low and lifts up. He raises the poor from the dust and lifts the beggar from the ash heap (dunghill), to set them among princes and make them inherit the throne of glory. It further emphasizes in that text that *"the pillars of the earth are the Lord's, and He has set the world upon them. He will guard the feet of His saints, But the wicked shall be silent in darkness. For by strength no man shall prevail"* (1 Samuel 2:8-9).

There are instructive points in those words that you should take note of. One, it is God, the all-powerful One, that does all these things. He is God— the all-powerful, all-knowing God! The whole earth belongs to Him; He fashioned this vast and wonderful universe and decides what things are done or accomplished in it. He created the people and everything in it. The Bible says God is worthy *"to receive glory and honor and power; For You created all things, And by Your will they exist and were created."* (Revelation 4:11). Everything created—including you—was made for His pleasure. You were not designed by God to succeed outside Him—nothing was. Everything was designed to find its fulfillment in God and by God. This is the God Factor.

God is the source of all true success and victory. The Bible records that the earth is the Lord's and its fullness thereof. It means that God is the connecting line to everything that exists within the earth. Whatever is the degree and magnitude of true success, God is the source. Without Him, nothing will exist. You need the One who kills and makes alive. Life and death are in God's hands. He decides who lives and who does not. You need the One that makes poor and makes rich. The Apostle Paul highlights the sovereignty of the providence of God when he says that "*So then it is* not of him who wills, nor of him who runs, but of God who shows mercy." (Romans 9:16).

This means that even when you try within your limited human means to reach your dream height by yourself, you will get frustrated by the outcome, until God steps in and comes to your rescue. Without Him, you would keep moving back and forth in a tiring rigmarole without any real progress.

Only God has the complete understanding of the purpose of our creation because He is the creator. It is just like the gadgets we purchase as humans, We can only trust the manufacturer of a gadget to give us an in-depth description of the full capacity of its functionality, because the manufacturer knows the makeup and every bit of the gadget, including its strengths and weaknesses. In the same way, God who created us knows us better than anyone else. He understands our nature; therefore, it is best we stay connected to Him for continual guidance on our journey to reaching the place of our prepared destiny. We will never be able to realize the full capacity and worth of our potentials if we do not remain aligned with God who is the Giver and Source of this potential. We may never attain fulfillment until we are fully acquainted with the source of our potential, God Almighty.

By strength shall no one prevail because no matter how much you apply your human efforts, energy, or resources, you will still not go far in the direction of God's will for your life. God owns and controls the universe and that is why people keep getting frustrated when they try to figure out things on their own. Some may have wisdom, but they do not end up being the best because they lack the God factor. Some eventually become the best in whatever they do but are brought down terribly by the vicissitudes of life. That is one way God confounds the proud and gives grace to the humble.

The text in 1 Samuel 2:8-9 also says that *"God will guide His saints."* As you make your journey through life, God intends to guide you. He is interested in your success and happiness, and He wants to lead you to the throne—to the place of divine fulfilment. But He must do it on His own terms. He is not just going to rubberstamp your decisions or actions.

Passport to Divine Support

He will guide His saints. Are you a saint? God's saints are those who have come into a relationship with Him; those who have surrendered their lives to Him. God will only lead those who have relinquished their right to lead themselves to Him. Have you made this decision? Have you surrendered your life to Him and accepted Him as Lord and Savior? It does not matter what your story is; it does not matter how many times you have fallen or been in the dungeon of your life. You can rise again if you surrender to the Lord completely. His ears and arms are wide open to receive your sincere cries of surrender. Just because you have fallen countless times does not mean that God cannot save you.

Numerous persons have had the dunghill experience and have risen to the throne by divine connection. There is a touching story of a missionary pastor that moved to a remote area in Africa to win souls for Christ. Somehow, the community was not in support of his new revival. So, his wife was killed in the process. This particular experience devastated him, and he never regained his faith back. He had led people to Christ during that time of revival, but he eventually gave up. He left the place alone, leaving his kids behind. He was given to alcohol for an awfully long time.

However, many years later, his daughter found him in a motel - reeking with alcohol - and helped him to surrender to Christ again. She explained to her father how a man who had given his life to Christ in one of his crusades had taken charge of his mission. He was taken for treatments, but he was already too damaged due to his reckless living. He made good use of the little time he had left. He made sure he picked up his cross from where he left it and continued that mission. Although he had wasted a lot of years, he chose to rise by connecting back to God. And God made his life beautiful again.

I want to assure you that your dunghill story is coming to an end; now is the time to break loose from whatever fetters might have tied you down. Commit yourself to God and allow Him to walk with you in every area of your life.

6

STAY CONNECTED TO YOUR SOURCE

"Recognize your dependence on God. As the days become dark and the nights become dreary, realize that there is a God who rules above."
—**Martin Luther King Jr.**

When your union with God becomes the most important thing in your life, it becomes easy to avoid every form of compromise. When you are in right standing with God, your spiritual sensitivity and reception will be sharpened. Your singleness of purpose in devotion to God provides you the ability to be constantly aware of His plans and intentions for you. You get the understanding of what He wants you to do and when He wants you to do it; where He wants you to go and what steps He wants you to take per season. You constantly receive directions through the Spirit of God when you make it a point of duty to constantly strengthen your connection and relationship with Him.

Whatever is God's purpose for your life, you can only depend on the Holy Spirit's help for the success of it. We are assured in 1 Corinthians 2:9-12 that God's provisions and plans for us supersede all the thoughts of any individual—beyond human's idea of best—and we can only get a full insight into this excellent plan God has for us by constantly yielding ourselves to understanding His ways and desires for our lives through His Spirit.

The need to constantly stay connected to God is also seen in Proverbs 2:5-6, which exhorts us to have absolute trust in God and not be overly confident in our own wisdom to enjoy the benefits of constant guidance. When you are connected to God as the true source of your strength, you become unstoppable. Whatever comes your way, you can be sure you will overcome because the One in whom you have placed your trust has never lost any battle. Being connected to God helps to uphold your spirit and helps you maintain the winning attitude, even when circumstances appear otherwise. This is because you get to constantly hear God's voice in every situation. This enables you to see what others cannot see.

An example from the Scriptures is Ruth, who chose to

remain with her mother-in-law despite Naomi's plea for her to return. Her devotedness to the God of Israel gave her the courage to look beyond the physical and insist on going with Naomi. Her singleness of purpose to serve the God of Israel guided her in making the right decision that appeared foolish in the sight of men. Indeed, the end-result of Ruth's decision proves to us that God guided her in deciding to follow Naomi when Orpah turned back. Her unrivaled devotion to the God of Israel earned her the honor of becoming one of the progenitors of Jesus Christ. God took her from the dunghill of sorrow and widowhood to the throne of eternal remembrance.

God does not rely on the circumstances surrounding us to fulfil His promises to us. Even when it appears that a situation is too difficult for success or breakthrough to be achieved, as long as you do His bidding and focus on Him and not the situation, you must remain strong and firm, no matter how much the winds blow, till you realize the fulfillment of that which He has promised you. With God, there is no such thing as late manifestation; He makes things beautiful in His time. He ensures our prosperity, success, and manifestation come in due season as we have it in Psalm 1:3, but it takes extraordinary grace to see things in the perspective of God when in seemingly impossible situations. This is why you cannot afford to be disconnected from God. He is the One who gives the promise, the One who has the perfect plan for the fulfillment of the promise, and the One who can give the extraordinary enabling power for its fulfillment.

Understand Your Identity

Not understanding who you are in Christ will limit you and hinder you from living in the knowledge of the rights and privileges you have in Him. When you understand your identity in Christ, it changes the way you reason and live. Unfortunately, one of the major reasons a lot of people end up not getting to their prepared place of destiny is because they suffer from an identity crisis. Many identify with problems, challenges, and limitations confronting them, rather than seeing themselves for who Christ says they are.

Of course, most of the negative things we identify ourselves with would have been true of us and were indeed true of us without Christ in our lives. Before we took up the privileged offer to be called the sons and daughters of God by forsaking our sinful ways and accepting Christ as our Savior, we were destined for destruction, despair, degradation, and eternal death. However, with Christ as our Redeemer, we have access to boundless privileges. Consequently, instead of death and destruction, which should have been the appropriate punishment for our sinful ways, we get to receive abundant and eternal life as a gracious gift for our repentance.

A proper picture of our new identity in Christ is revealed

in 2 Corinthians 5:17: "*Therefore, if anyone is in Christ, he is a new creation; old things have passed away; behold, all things have become new.*" Being believers affords us the benefits of a new life in Christ. There are so many examples of people in the Scripture who had a negative identity of themselves. They lived as ordinary people, with no vision, purpose, or direction; but their lives took a remarkable turn when God made them understand who He had truly purposed them to be.

Gideon was one of such. He had thought of himself as a nonentity and had been so afraid of the Midianites that he had to hide inside a winepress to thresh his wheat. He was living in fear and terror of the enemy, not realizing that God had purposed him to be a terror to the enemy instead. He did not realize this until the day the angel of the Lord appeared to him to reveal his true identity by declaring to him in Judges 6:12, "*The Lord is with you, you mighty man of valor!*" When Gideon finally got to see himself the way God saw him, he then began to live fully in his divine purpose as a deliverer of Israel.

In Christ lies the identity that can enable us to be the absolute best and reach our prepared place of destiny fulfillment. So when the devil whispers lies of incompleteness and unworthiness, we can cut him off with the revelation of our identity in Colossians 2:10, that we have been made complete in Christ. When he whispers lies of being forsaken by God, we can silence him with the assurance of our goodly heritage in Ephesians 1:18. When he whispers lies of failure and defeat to you, you can hush him with your true identity of being more than a conqueror in Christ (Romans 8:37).

2 Timothy 1:7 assures us of power, love, and sound mind in Christ; therefore it is a given that we can do all things through Christ's strength. Understanding your identity in Christ will give strength and stability to your Christian faith, thus equipping you with the power and authority needed to ascend the throne of your prepared destiny.

Act on the Word

God has given us so many instructions in His Word that guarantee our victorious sailing through life. However, it is one thing to know these instructions and quite another to do them. In Joshua 1:8, the Lord commands that we fill our mouth and heart with His words, while ensuring that we do all that we are instructed to do, so as to have good success.

Just as every new product purchased has a manual that guides its use, the Bible is the God-given manual for our lives. When a product is being used without considering what the owner's manual says, problems are inevitable. Myles Munroe puts it this way: "When purpose is unknown, abuse is inevitable". Therefore, follow divine instructions to avoid a life of confusion and crisis.

Prayer is the Master Key

Prayer is the key that opens impossible doors. The effect of prayer in a person's life cannot be overemphasized. He that kneels before God will stand before anybody. God is the creator, and He knows what is best for us. This is why we should not fail to call on Him in and out of trouble. He encourages us with His Word in James 5:16, "*The effective, fervent prayer of a righteous man avails much.*"

The Holy Scripture is replete with examples of heroes of faith who prayed, and things changed. Elijah prayed and rain fell, Joshua prayed, and the course of nature changed, Daniel prayed and there was deliverance, Esther prayed and there was liberation, Moses prayed and the Red Sea parted. Jesus also called on God and many miracles followed His ministry.

Therefore, pray like your life depends on it because it does. Soon, you will see your burdens and obstacles melting away. If you have faith as a grain of mustard seed, you will command the mountain to be removed and it will go and nothing shall be impossible unto you, so says the word of God. So, command that very challenge that seeks to limit your life and it will flee!

7

KEY STEPS TO REACHING THE THRONE

"Destiny is no matter of chance. It is a matter of choice. It is not a thing to be waited for, it is a thing to be achieved."
- Williams Jennings Bryan

The above quote could not have been better said. As children of God, we have God's sure promises that should fill us with joy and assurance of a successful and fulfilled life. In Jeremiah 29:11, for instance, the Lord assures us that His thoughts towards us are always thoughts of peace and not of evil. Well, yes, He sure was not mincing words when He said that.

Unfortunately, many believers seem to have taken such promises of God to mean that success and destiny will happen to them by chance. They take no intentional steps or make no intentional moves in getting to the throne that God has assured them. Yes, the throne is ours; it is a promise made to us by our heavenly Father, but it does not come cheap, neither does it come by mere luck.

Discover Your Purpose

Purpose is both the goalpost and anchor of destiny. Without clarity of purpose, you would be easily swept along by the storms and other distractions of life. The ability to identify your purpose will make it possible for you to live and thrive. How can you know what your destiny entails if you lack an understanding of the purpose for which God created you?

For every living soul on earth, there is a divine purpose, irrespective of the circumstances surrounding our birth or background. Your purpose is the core essence of your existence. It is meant to guide your decisions, influence your behavior, shape your goals, give you a sense of direction, and thereby forming an overall definition of your life.

When you can identify the "why" of your existence and your unique attributes, you will find the passion to sail through the course of your destiny. In the words of Terry Orlick, "The heart of human excellence often begins to beat when you discover a pursuit that absorbs you, frees you, challenges you or gives you a sense of meaning, joy or passion."

Usually, the purpose for which God created you might not necessarily revolve around only the things you are fond of or take pleasure in alone; it could be greater and appear like things beyond your natural capability; after all, it is all about how God has chosen or called you to impact the world.

Nature of Purpose

Many people have a wrong notion about what living a life of purpose really means. If you think a purposeful or successful life is determined by wealth accumulated, power attained or status in society, then you are wrong. There are enough examples of people who, although appear to have acquired great wealth and success in life, still feel like something is missing in their lives. Ever wondered why some famous people end up committing suicide or dying of drug overdose even when it appears they have the "perfect" life?

As individuals, our God-given purposes and assignments in life differ. We all cannot always head in the same direction. In Paul's letter to the Ephesians, he talked about the diversity of assignments and purposes (Ephesians 4:11-13). He particularly noted in verse 7 that, for the different purposes that God has designed for us, there is a fuel called grace (or divine empowerment) to maximize, do exploits, and become fulfilled by it. Simply put, there is no God-given ability or calling that is insignificant. God has designed it in such a way that whatever gift or talent you have is definitely worth pursuing and investing in.

Rhythms of Purpose

It is important to note that the dynamics of life's experiences as we grow and move on to different phases of life can help us to gain clarity about our life's purpose. As our priorities evolve and we experience various transitions in life's journey, it will, to a large extent, help to define, refine, and solidify our purpose.

Take, for example, a young girl who has had things easy and sweet all her life. Her parents are always there, supporting her every step of the way. Then out of the blues, she loses both parents to a car accident. The experience will be devastating, no doubt. She will be made to transit to a new phase of life she never rehearsed for, a phase no longer nice and easy.

For such a girl, as she begins the journey on the sharp turn her life has taken, many would assume she will probably be lost, searching for how to make meaning of her life, But here is the good thing about discovering purpose: whatever it is she eventually makes of her life, her experiences and journey sure would not be a smooth sail; but it would prepare her to see a need to be a source of inspiration and encouragement to others when she finally pulls through herself. This picture of what she hopes to be, against all odds, will keep her pressing on. Experiences differ, but often, a lot of people have had to discover a new reason for living, birthed by devastating experiences.

You should also understand that fulfilling life's purpose goes beyond self-gratification. It is about your contribution to the world and how you have been chosen to impact it with your gifts. A gift could appear "little" or grand, but the most important thing is that it gives you a sense of direction and ultimate fulfilment. Understand however that in fulfilling life's purpose, we only get one shot at this. There are no rehearsals, it is only one life. It is our duty to make the most of it.

The following will guide you toward living a purposeful life:

1. Find your passion: Living a life of purpose requires that you have a reason to wake up each morning, eager to face the new day. When you are passionate about something, it will come with an inner drive that will serve as a propelling force to make you willingly invest your time, energy, and resources into it. It becomes something you care for deeply, pursue with fervor, and fight for with every ounce of you.

2. Discover your talent: There's no one created without an innate ability that makes them unique from others. The challenge with some people usually is that their environment and circumstances do not allow them to explore these abilities. It is quite easy for some people to discover these innate abilities called talents early enough to pursue them with passion, while some others do not. This is not in any way to say that there are people with no talent; far from it. If you are one of those who seem not to have a clear idea of what their talent really is, understand that it does not mean you lack it. There is always something you love to do naturally; something that finds expression through you with no struggle.

What confuses most people when it comes to discovering their talent is their narrow understanding of what a talent is. Many limits it to something only about music, dance, handicrafts, or the arts. It is beyond these, however. It is actually anything you are naturally good at.

Furthermore, discovering your talent is not as rigorous or difficult as you may think. That you have not been able to identify it before now does not mean you have to go through some daunting exercises or some sort of drilling to discover it. It has always been there and oftentimes, not having been able to discover it is due to our inability to pay attention to its workings.

If you are yet to identify your talent for whatever reason, take some time out for self-reflection. Seek divine inspiration by praying about it, and pay attention to your natural strengths. In Jeremiah 1:5, which we read earlier, we have an assurance that there is no one created without a purpose and some measure of grace to fulfill that purpose:

"Before I formed you in the womb I knew you; Before you were born I sanctified you; I ordained you a prophet to the nations."

God has deposited something in you; He has a purpose for you to fulfill on this earth. Reflect on what you are usually naturally inclined and instinctively drawn towards. No gift is insignificant or less important compared to another. That it is not highly esteemed in a place or by some group of people does not make it irrelevant or invalid. Whatever dream your talent has inspired in you remains valid, for it was put in you by God.

At the beginning, you may not fully understand God's total plan, the full picture of what God has in store; but as you yield yourself to Him continually and become more open in your heart to his leadings and direction, He unfolds more of His plans to you.

It is very possible to attain a successful height in life and still be filled with pangs of unfulfillment, This is because fulfillment only comes with living in the purpose for which you were created. Simply put, you can do many great things but remain unfulfilled because you have not lived your life for the purpose for which you were created. Have you ever wondered why many seemingly successful people in different fields of endeavors still end up in misery and despair? Your throne of destiny is that place prepared for you in the sphere which you have been chosen to impact. If you do not get to discover your purpose, you will be clueless as to what path to tread to reach there. As much as God has a good plan for you, He also needs you to cooperate with Him by abiding by His precepts.

3. Avoid negativity: We all can in one way or the other identify certain things in our lives that make us feel miserable. Many of us are yoked with the belief that those things are destined to be our lot—a cross we have been condemned to bear—and there is nothing we can do about it, except to live on with the mess. Well, it will be liberating for you to know that there is something you can do about it. The first step is identifying the things that make you miserable. It could be a bad relationship; people you are surrounded with or experiences you had growing up. Once you have been able to identify them, the next step is to confront them. By taking courage to get rid of all forms of negativity in your life, it will usher in a feeling of liberation in your soul and you will be equipped with courage for a fresh start as you set out to fulfill your purpose.

4. Be intentional: The quality of your life is largely dependent on how purposeful your life's journey is. It is by this that you truly get to enjoy life and have a deep inspirational satisfaction for living. The key to this is being intentional about growth and always getting better than who you used to be.

Nobody gets to the pinnacle of success or peak of destiny

fulfillment by mere happenstance. To fulfill destiny, there is a constant need for you to be strategically motivated to really pursue the cause. While it is imperative to discover the purpose for which you are created, it is equally important to take practical and intentional steps to help bring this to fulfillment.

The first, most important intentional step to be taken is to spend time alone with God, commune with Him, express your total reliance and dependence on Him as the core of your existence. Stay put to listen to him as He gives you a clear definition of your purpose. Take note however, that after you might have received His affirmation for the purpose of your creation, there is yet more work to be done; there is a need for action plans to be developed and pursued. Fulfillment of big visions emanates from a series of small decisions. To help you make the right decisions at crucial moments of your life, one important intentional step you can take is to write down your vision, as well as the revelations, promises and instructions given by God during your solemn times of communion with Him to help guard your pursuit and help you stay on track accurately towards the defined goal He has given to you.

5. Be teachable: There is no champion without a coach; therefore, whatever height you hope to attain in life, there is a need for you to be ever ready to learn, unlearn and relearn. Someone with a teachable spirit will be quick to take to corrections and not try to always put up a defense for their misdeeds. There is hardly anyone who has made their mark in any field of endeavor, that rose to that position all by themselves without training and mentoring from someone they could look up to. Esther had Mordecai as her mentor, while Elisha submitted to Elijah as his mentor. These two people who were recorded in the scriptures to have done great exploits have one thing in common - complete devotion to being taught.

6. Develop yourself: A lot of people believe it is the devil working against them if they do not get a job or benefit from some other opportunities. However, more often than not, it is because they lack the required qualification for that position. Proverbs 22:29 makes us to understand that someone diligent in his business will stand before kings and not mere men. This verse of Scripture does not say someone diligent in another's business but his own. So, do not be a busybody or a Jack of all trades, doing so many things but doing nothing. Get busy with things that give you an edge over your peers and even your seniors. Even Scripture teaches us to study to be approved. How much study have you given yourself to that will make you stand out? Invest in your future and you will always be grateful you did.

7. Believe in yourself: How far you go in life depends on how far you see yourself going. If you do not believe in yourself, then you are your greatest obstacle. What makes you think you cannot get to the throne? Do you believe it is your background, friends, or some physical limitations? Do not let these factors define your future. Tim Rettig opines that your belief system is the invisible force behind your behavior. In other words, you act out your beliefs. Therefore, if you do not believe in yourself, your life will let out a stench of negativity.

Believe that you can make anything possible. It is in your hands to decide your future, not in the hands of your parents or friends. Remember, the person who believes some things are impossible paves the way for another person who believes he or she can do everything they want to do. So, take the bull by the horn and make positive confessions concerning your life.

8. Use the vehicle of people: As much as God does not depend on anyone to do what He has to do; He still uses people as instruments to accomplish His purposes. The only caveat is that no one is indispensable to God. God will not come down literally from heaven to help you get to your prepared place of destiny, but He uses people. He often raises people and networks us with them at different stages of our lives to help us get to where He has purposed to take us.

Truly, God has diverse ways of making His will known to His children, but you must understand that one of the major ways God speaks to his children is through godly counsels. He does this by bringing people who will offer godly counsels your way. The Bible says in Proverbs 13:20: "*He who walks with wise men will be wise, But the companion of fools will be destroyed.*" The kind of people you are surrounded with will go a long way in determining how far you can go on the journey to destiny, and will most certainly shape the outcome of your life.

Certain relationships are toxic for the fulfillment of your destiny; such relationships are detrimental to your God-given assignment. If you are surrounded by people who are full of divine insight, they will aid your ascension to the throne; but if you are surrounded by people who are full of self-wisdom and self-conceit, you most likely will deviate from the path that will lead to the prepared place of destiny fulfillment. In other words, there is a need to be mindful of the kind of people you allow to be involved in your life.

You most certainly cannot accomplish much without having a relationship with people, as the popular saying goes, "a forest cannot make a tree". But you just have to be sure you are surrounded by people who have the mind of God. People whom God will choose to use to help us fulfill our destiny and purpose will not come as angels from heaven; they come in form of families, pastors, colleagues, friends, life coaches, mentors, and sometimes, strangers.

Looking at the life of Esther, have you ever wondered

what could have become of her if she had not listened to Mordecai's instruction about not revealing who her people or family were? Did you ever wonder what would have become of the nation of Israel in Esther's time if she had not stood up for her people by daring to go against the rules binding the maidens in the palace? At every instance, Esther was yielded enough to listen to wise counsel and humble enough to obey instructions.

Many people today believe that when they get to a certain age or level in life, they do not need to submit to the authority of anyone again, not even their parents or spiritual leaders. They ignore wise counsel and simply make decisions with no regard for knowing the mind of God concerning steps to be taken. Such people are like Samson. If Samson had listened to his parents about not taking a wife from among the Philistines, he would not have ended his ministerial journey in the camp of the enemy. He would have lived longer, conquering nations, delivering Israel, and being their judge in a version that would never have been replicated in history.

There is no record of any other individual who wielded such physical strength like that of Samson, but he cut short his journey to the throne that God had prepared for him by disregarding godly counsel and trivializing the position of authority his parents had over him. If you are the kind of person always wants to have his or her way, self-confident and self-opinionated, there is every possibility you may not get to the throne; but if it happens that you get there, you certainly will not be able to operate in the fullness of God's original design.

There is also the need to be conscious of certain people God will bring your way as destiny helpers. They are to help make up for your deficiencies or limitations. Sometimes, such people are like strangers or people who appear not to be of much relevance to us. As a result, there is always a tendency to look down on them. Consider the case of Naaman, the great general in the scripture who was plagued with leprosy. He was able to get his healing as a result of the recommendation made to him by his maidservant. Ever wondered what would have become of him if he had disregarded the maid's recommendation to visit Prophet Elisha for his healing? He sure would have died in that leprosy.

Sometimes, the help we need may not come from the high and mighty. It could come from people who can be seen as low to us in rank or social status. When we ask for God's intervention, we are not to expect literal manna falling from heaven as it happened in the wilderness for the children of Israel. God uses men as instruments to bring about the fulfillment of His promises.

8

CONQUERING OBSTACLES TO THE THRONE

"Obstacles do not have to stop you. If you run into a wall, do not turn around and give up. Figure out how to climb it, go through it or work around it."

— **Michael Jordan**

"I know you are hungry, and, for that fact, I will give you some of my pottage - but on one condition", Jacob said. With a tone of frustration, Esau replied, "What could you possibly want, little man? "You know you are the firstborn son of our father, Isaac; I want you to give me that slot and the privileges that come with it", Jacob replied immediately. "Done, just do not ask me any *further questions and give me the pottage before I die."* Esau replied. Just to be sure his request was adequately adhered to, Jacob made Esau take an oath (Genesis 25:27-34).

What happened here? Esau had just sold his birthright without giving it much thought! And by the time he realized what he had done, the blessing that should have been his had been long gone, never to be regained, even after he sought it with tears of regret (Hebrews 12:17). In relation to this tragic incident, it is essential that we examine three pertinent questions here. First, what are the obstacles faced by people on their way to the throne? Second, why are there obstacles in the first place? And third, how can these obstacles be conquered?

Challenges are a particularly important part of human life. Job 14:1 portrays human life on earth as full of trouble. This suggests that as long as we remain flesh and blood, we cannot escape challenges. These challenges spring from different aspects of life and they affect every human. However, for children of God, our case is peculiar in two ways. First is that being special people, Satan deliberately attacks us with targeted challenges, which could manifest in diverse forms. Secondly and more importantly, God uses every challenge we face to bless and uplift us.

It must be emphasized, though, that the eventual outcomes of our challenges largely depend on how we approach them.

The case of Esau and Jacob, which we explored earlier, is very instructive here. Esau allowed the temporary pangs of hunger to make him behave irrationally and thereby lose something of eternal worth.

Essentially, then, challenges, if handled positively, will become stepping stones for the challenged; but if handled otherwise, can end in more troubles and traumas. Before challenges can be overcome, they must be identified.

Decisive Crossroads

Let me highlight some of the challenges that often constitute a barrier to reaching the throne.

1. Bleak background

Home is where the foundation of a child's future is laid before other institutions and influences come into play. A family where the parents have given up trying to succeed, simply because things have never worked well for them will pose a major challenge for anyone aspiring to succeed. Chances are that a child that grows up in such an environment will be surrounded by so much negativity and pessimism.

The scripture however reveals that *"weeping may endure for a night but joy comes in the morning"* (Psalm 30:5). This reminds us that even though problems are inevitable, they cannot be present much longer than God wants them to and there will, most definitely, be a time of victory.

Jabez, in 1 Chronicles 4:9-10, was born in sorrow, and that brought about his name. Ordinarily, he could have decided to remain at that level but he decided to change the conventional order of things in his family. He went to God and requested a change and Scripture records that God granted him that which he requested.

Jabez had come to the knowledge of the truth of God's outstretched arm being available at all times He is called upon, as well as His willingness to help. He did not delay in calling upon the One that knows the end from the beginning. I believe if Jabez were here today and he is approached for advice on an issue similar to the one he passed through, he would have told the concerned individual: "Do not remain there, go to God."

Obstacles from the home or family background still constitute a major barrier to many people today. But the question is, what do you do about it? Do you just sit, complain, and watch it blossom, or will you rise above it and climb out? Make the wise decision!

2. Peer influence

Richelle E. Goodrich once said, "*Do not underestimate the power of friendship. Those bonds are stitches that close up the holes you might otherwise fall through*" Friendships are important relationships throughout a person's lifespan, which is why choosing friends should not be done casually. Friendship is influence and it happens both ways. "Show me your friend and I'll tell you who you are" is an old maxim used to relay the importance of friendship.

The company one keeps can determine how far one goes in life. Simply put, when you have someone as a friend, he can lift you up or pull you down. This is why someone with a mind to go past average will make friends with people that have distinctions, so he will be drawn up.

The story of David and Jonathan in the Bible teaches great lessons about friendship. David's life was in danger because Jonathan's father, Saul, wanted to kill him. But what did Jonathan do? He protected David without his father's knowledge because he knew his father's plots were evil. Saul was after David because he had done more exploits than him by killing Goliath. Jonathan, being a true friend lifted David.

The reverse is the case in another story in Scripture. Amnon had a friend, named Jonadab, who he talked to about different things happening in his life. At a particular time, Amnon developed a destructive lust for his sister and discussed it with his supposed friend. Jonadab not only encouraged him to satisfy his lust but also gave him tips on how to go about it. Amnon followed these steps and defiled his sister. Absalom, the brother of Tamar (the defiled lady), heard about it and remained angry until the day he killed Amnon. At the time of Amnon's death, Jonadab was nowhere to be found. He had led his friend to his death and disappeared when the consequence came crawling. While Jonathan led David to the top, Jonadab led Amnon to his death.

This portrays the importance of having friends that are positive builders, not destroyers. When someone wants to uphold what is right and he has principles that help him keep to that and his closest friend is someone that opposes all he stands for, gradually, those principles begin to drop and before he realizes, he has lost all sense of uprightness.

God gives a warning in 1 Corinthians 15:33, *"Evil communication corrupts good manners"*. This means that good manners are sustained by good communication. Also, before a person takes the slot of a friend to you, you must make sure he is in the same lane and wants to move higher or even better than you so you do not end up going back into a tunnel you have almost climbed out of. Choose your friends wisely.

3. Quick Gratification

"I want it now – like, right now! I do not want to hear what anyone wants to tell me. Just give it to me!" These must have been the words in the mouth of the prodigal son when he requested for his part of his father's wealth. Well, he got it but in no time, it was gone and he returned home empty. His father could not turn his back on him, so he accepted him. But one thing remained - he had squandered his inheritance. The consequence of dwelling on the "NOW" is more dangerous than the reason for the choice.

The example of Esau is also pertinent here. He was hungry; Jacob had food to share but he requested something in return. Esau did not hesitate to give him that which he requested, his birthright. And for some sort of assurance requested by Jacob, Esau swore and God took note. Yes, Esau got the food but what he lost was far beyond the food he got. Esau must have wished he did not eat that food that day because he would still have had his place as the firstborn son of his father; but he mortgaged it all because of impatience.

This is what happens when we allow feelings to consume us to make hasty decisions. If Esau had thought more about the implication of the decision he was about to make, he might have rejected the food and gone to ask his mother for his meal but he made it seem like if he did not eat Jacob's food at that moment, he would die immediately.

The children of Israel, in Exodus 16:2-3, murmured against Moses and Aaron because they had nothing to eat in the wilderness. They were happy about their deliverance from bondage but when they were faced with another challenge, they forgot the God who had delivered them and focused on what they had been eating in Egypt. These people were always so focused on their present circumstances that they forgot that the God who had done many wonderful things for them in the past could do so many more in the present. They were ever impatient in their dealings with God.

This experience is some people's reality. They want to get rich quick, get that job quick, get married quick, and so on. And this continues to make them take regrettable steps. The Scripture has clearly the aftermath of the "get-rich-quick" syndrome in 1 Timothy 6:9 thus: "*But those who desire to be rich fall into temptation and a snare, and into many foolish and harmful lusts which drown men in destruction and perdition.*" In verse 10, the Scripture further explains that because of the love of money, a lot of people have done terrible things that have caused them untold sorrow and regrets.

Therefore, desiring riches is not bad in itself but when a person has been consumed by the "NOW" factor that he forgets that there is a process to acquire wealth in a godly way and dabbles into questionable practices, he will definitely face the consequences.

4. Defeatist Attitude

God will direct your life, only if you let Him. This means that we are largely in control of our lives. Even in the Scripture, God makes it clear that people have to decide for Him by themselves. He also tells us that He has set before us life and death, but because of His thoughts of peace towards us, He implores everyone to choose life that we may live (Deuteronomy 30:19).

You become an obstacle to YOU when YOU do not believe anything good can come out of YOU. As a child of God, there is a power that works in you through your Father in heaven, and He wants you to use that power in all situations. People generally believed that nothing good could come out of Nazareth but that backwater town birthed our Savior, Jesus Christ. A lot of people may believe you cannot achieve much, but what do you think about yourself? Do you believe them and decide to remain at the base level or do you believe what your Creator has said and operate in that light?

Leon brown said you have the power within yourself to make anything possible; therefore, you must diminish the doubt and ignite the self-belief. You are capable of amazing things; so, believe in yourself and believe what your Father has said concerning you and walk in it because that will become your reality.

5. Discouragement

"It's not working; I have tried it countless times". This could be your thought right now. Thomas Edison did not give up on trying to make the light bulb a reality. According to reports, he tried about 1000 times before it worked. If you could advise him way before he tried it the 400th time, perhaps you would have told him to go do something different with his life because the bulb idea would not work. Edison must have understood that hard work with a whole lot of perseverance pays off.

Sometimes, things do not work at the time you want them to. This should not bring discouragement; it should only make you try harder. God may be watching to see how determined and persistent you can be to bring your idea to reality.

6. Fear of Failure

Failure is not the opposite of success; it is a part of success. All successful people have stories of failure as well. Failure does not mean that it is all over for you or your dream. Failure only becomes fatal when you stop trying. It is not a dead-end until you make it one. Failure should even be appreciated because it helps you see your mistakes and repeating the same is impossible. So, when you fail, learn from it, pick up yourself, and do it again.

When you are scared of failing, it hinders you from trying, and you can hardly go far if you do not try. Michael Jordan says, "*I can accept failure; everyone fails at something, but I cannot accept not trying*". This is the truth. Everyone you see in the spotlight today has failed at something but they did not let that failure affect their future.

Therefore, you should not be scared to fail because it has a way of lifting you above your present level. Failure teaches lessons that make you better; it leaves you better than it met you. In Romans 5:3-5 Paul says *"And not only that, but we also glory in tribulations, knowing that tribulation produces perseverance; and perseverance, character; and character, hope. Now hope does not disappoint, because the love of God has been poured out in our hearts by the Holy Spirit who was given to us."* From this passage, Paul explains the importance of tribulations; it works to put in us virtues like patience, experience, and hope, which will count in the long run as we proceed on life's journey. Therefore, when failure comes, do not think the world has come to an end for you but have a positive mindset towards it and be open to learning.

7. Low Self-esteem

David did not consider his size when he faced Goliath. He knew he did not have the looks of a warrior but his God was bigger and greater than Goliath and he would not let anyone defy God's people. He was not bothered when the other warriors said, "You have never been in a battle; he has been fighting since his youth. Are you crazy?" Even Goliath called him a small boy and laughed him to scorn but David was not scared at all; all he had in his mind was that his God would help him to defeat the uncircumcised philistine.

Self-esteem, according to Wikipedia, is an individual's subjective evaluation of their worth. In other words, this means how you view yourself. It is your overall sense of self-worth or personal value. Do you think you can amount to anything? Do you believe you can do better than you are now? Belief in yourself and your ability goes a long way in determining how far you go in life's journey. You may have made a lot of mistakes in the past but you are not your mistakes, they are what you did not who you are. You have been criticizing yourself for years and it has not worked to bring forth any positive result. Try approving of yourself and see what happens. You deserve your love and affection; let nobody tell you otherwise.

Love yourself with everything in you because it is the way you see yourself that people will see you. It is exceedingly difficult to stop people who believe they can do anything they set their minds to do. Sometimes, you do not know you can do some things except you try to do them and you see what you have bottled up over the years. The psalmist in Scripture says that though he is besieged by an army, his heart will not fear; though a war breaks out against him, even then will he be confident (Psalm 27:3). Such self-belief! The psalmist understood how much belief in oneself can move him to do the "supposed" impossible.

Make sure you believe in yourself and what God has said concerning you. Never permit anything that will reduce your self-worth because it can affect your life. Be as positive as you can be.

8. Negative Habits

A habit is a routine of behavior that is repeated regularly and tends to occur subconsciously. Habits are easy to pick up but difficult to drop. When you decide to change your habits, then life can take a different turn for you. Habits can make you or break you, and as much as motivation gets you started on your journey to the throne, it is your habits that will keep you going. Pick up habits that are meant for the throne and do away with those that keep the throne at a distance.

Why have obstacles anyway? I know this may be the question bugging your mind. God created humans to enjoy the works of His hands but since the Fall in Genesis 3, the original intention of God changed and wickedness crept into the world. In Genesis 6:5, God saw that the world had been so consumed in wickedness that the thoughts of people's hearts were continually evil. As initially conceived by God, life was originally meant to be a bed of roses. But when Adam decided to trade the roses for an eye-opening apple, it led to the downfall of humanity. These obstacles are a product of the wickedness inherent in human nature.

If you have overcome a challenge before, you would understand that if they are handled well, they make you better; they move you to a higher echelon. Obstacles mold, instruct, strengthen, help us prioritize, and increase our creativity. When obstacles come your way, you should be happy about them because you know you will overcome and you are coming out better. Remember, there is no victory without a fight. So, prepare to fight because victory is assured. A general in the army is not celebrated because he sits down in the office but because he has beheld war and he has come out victorious.

So far, we have explored some obstacles that can pose a threat to your reaching the throne prepared for you, but I have also highlighted the possibility and process of overcoming them. Overcoming obstacles, both internal and external, is very possible because our heavenly Father has brought to our understanding that He will not allow challenges we cannot bear to come our way (1 Corinthians 10:13). God is faithful enough to make a way of escape for us.

9

SEE IT, HAVE IT

""For as he thinks in his heart, so is he"
—Proverbs 23:7

A practical dreamer will always progress, no matter how tough the situation is. Once your mind can conceive an idea, then you can achieve it, no matter how difficult the idea might seem. You can have whatever you dream of if you diligently walk the path.

Success is not given to anyone; you have to work hard to achieve it. However, having a vision strengthens your resolve and keeps driving you forward to achieve the set goal. Vision is very crucial for success to be achieved. A visionless person cannot have anything with just wishful thinking. Dreams come true when we press forward by playing our part in making sure it becomes a reality.

Power of the Mind

To achieve your dream and become what God has destined you to be, the journey must begin in your mind. If you cannot imagine your destination, then you cannot get there. David Cuschieri once said, "*The mind is a powerful force. It can enslave us or empower us. It can plunge us into the depths of mystery or take us to the heights of ecstasy. Learn to use the power wisely.*"

The most powerful tool any human possesses is the mind. It is deep and inexhaustible; it has the power to create and to destroy. As human, you must learn to build your mind towards greatness. Every idea that has changed the world at one time or another was first birthed in the mind. It can be used to attain success or it can plunge you deep into failure. When you do not master the way your mind works, then you might never reach your full potential. A sage said, "A man is but the product of his thoughts; what he thinks, he becomes." Indeed, you reflect what goes on in your mind.

The mind works hand in hand with your imagination, and can create whatever you want it to: opportunities, failure, success, obstacles, happiness, wealth, industrious ideas, just name it. When you pay extra attention to the mind and learn how to focus, you will go extremely far. The power of the mind, when used positively, gives you a renewed sense of purpose, a burning desire to do something worthwhile, and an assurance that nothing is impossible. Thomas Edison invented the electric bulb and today, it has become a necessity for everyone; this dream however started in his mind. He failed several times, but because he believed in the power of his mind, he kept at it and as a result, his name can never be erased in history.

Once you learn how to explore your mind positively, you are on the pathway to achieving the impossible. And when the mind is effective and active, it can birth great visions.

Picture Your Future

Never underestimate the power of vision. According to Kenneth Labich, McDonald's founder, Ray Kroc *"pictured his empire in his mind long before it existed, and he saw how to get there. He invented the company motto- 'Quality, service, cleanliness and value. - And kept repeating it to employees for the rest of his life"*

The Bible says in Proverbs 29:18 (KJV), *"Where there is no vision, the people perish; but he that keepeth the law, happy is he."* This scripture is true; a visionless person will most likely end up in the ditch. In life, you can only go as far as your vision. When you have a limited vision, then your achievements will equally be limited. Understanding this is the power of vision. Vision changes the world, when there is a vision, be rest assured that there will surely be a way.

In Genesis 13: 14-15, God said unto Abraham, "...*for all the land which you see I give to you and your descendants forever.*" The emphasis here is how far Abraham could see; he was going to have as much as he could see! This indicates the power of vision. So many persons limit themselves; they are afraid to dream big and take bold steps.

Faith Your Fear to Death

One major enemy of vision is fear. No matter how great a vision is, you must not be too afraid to get it started. Instead of being fearful, learn to do it afraid. Truth is, oftentimes when you dream of great ideas, there is a subtle feeling of fear, which makes you feel it cannot be attained. You must learn to kill fear and bring the vision to life. No matter how beautiful a vision is, if it is not acted upon, it will never come to life.

No matter how big or great a vision is, it can definitely come to pass. You need to have faith in yourself and believe that nothing is impossible. Self-belief is very essential; it helps to fuel your faith and keeps you going when no one believes in your vision. It helps you sail through challenging situations and gives you hope of possibility. For every vision to be attainable, you need to believe in yourself and your dream. Self-belief helps positivity and possibility thrive, even in tough environments.

Strategize Your Triumph

"Vision is the art of seeing what is invisible to others," said Jonathan Swift. A vision is like a dream before it can be achieved, you will need to plan how you want to make it a reality. But without a vision, there is no reason to plan. You are the sole pilot of your destiny. When you have a clear vision of where you are going, it becomes easy to navigate your path despite the challenges that will come.

In the biblical story of Joseph, he had a dream and even though it felt like a mere dream to his brothers, he held on to it and trusted God to bring it to fruition. Joseph never lost sight of his destination; he had a picture of it and that was bigger than all the challenges he had to go through. Remember, he was thrown in a pit, was sold as a slave to Potiphar, and he was even thrown into prison for an offense he did not commit. Despite the pressing challenges around him, he did not lose sight of his dream. He visualized his end goal and eventually, it came to pass.

There is this saying that you are what you think. If you can dream it, you can definitely have it. Whatever the mind can conceive can be achieved, but a visionless mind can never achieve anything meaningful. Such a person can be likened to a weak branch that is easily tossed about by the wind. You will land where others want you to. However, when you have a picture of where you are going in mind, you cannot be led astray; you will not follow the crowd or be easily tossed about. As Christians, the fact that we can visualize our destination, which is heaven, helps to constantly keep us on track. A believer can endure whatever challenge; because he knows, heaven is more than a reward to anyone who makes it there.

Every example we need to navigate through life's part can be seen in the Scripture. Search the Scripture, and you will find that God never worked with visionless people. The twelve disciples of Jesus were hardworking, diligent, and dutiful people, who would not run at the sight of a little challenge. When Jesus met Peter, he was busy fishing. The Bible recorded that he had toiled all night to no avail. This means he labored all through the night with his partners trying to catch fishes in the river. He was not a man without vision or focus. Christ met him at his duty post and the story changed.

Other examples in the Bible include Paul, Matthew, and many others; they were people Jesus found at their duty posts. Paul (previously Saul) was an ardent persecutor of the church. His vision was to bring as many believers as possible to prison and he was doing everything in his power to ensure that Christians were persecuted and jailed. It was while on this path Jesus met him and the story changed. His vision changed from punishing believers to depopulating the kingdom of Satan and bringing as many to the kingdom of God. Paul was willing to lay down his life for the cause of the Gospel because he could visualize his destination. The same applies to Stephen and every other disciple of Christ.

Also, the story of Joshua and Caleb is told in the Old Testament. It is recorded that Moses sent out twelve men to spy the land of Canaan. Ten of the twelve spies came back bearing bad news, but two of them came back with hope and a renewed vision. Joshua and Caleb saw the good in the land; they saw beyond the seemingly obvious challenge and assured the people of having the land. They saw it, and it became theirs at the end. Remember, these two were the only ones who were privileged to enter Canaan land in their generation. This was because they had hope and believed in what they saw.

The journey from the dunghill to the throne requires hard work, persistence, and understanding. It takes people who are ready to take the journey, people who know what they are doing, people who are dedicated and focused, not people without a sense of purpose and direction. Anyone who is not ready to pay the price will not get to the throne. A lot of persons do not make use of the opportunity around them; they will rather give excuses for not doing what should be done. This set of people will move from the throne to the dunghill. An example is given in the bible to illustrate this better.

The story of the prodigal son resonates with everyone. It depicts the life of someone who moved from the throne to the dunghill. The son left the comfort of his home in search of ease and a so-called comfortable life. He became entangled with worldly things and ended up spending lavishly, without giving a thought for the morrow. In a short while, he exhausted his source of livelihood in a strange land. When he could not find something to do, he started working at a pig farm and was even eating food meant for pigs.

This story depicts the lifestyle of a visionless person. He drastically moved from the throne to the dunghill. He did not have a set goal; he did not have a picture of the kind of future he wanted. As a result, he wasted the resources he had, and he had to live with the consequences until he came to his senses. His story would have ended up even worse if he did not retrace his steps his source.

The moral of this story is that, as one who wants to inherit the throne, you cannot afford to live carelessly like those without a sense of purpose and direction. The prodigal son left his father without any sense of direction and he came back with nothing.

It is essential that we do an in-depth check of our lives and achievements regularly. I look back at my life and try to see how far I have come and how well I am doing; this helps me to strategize on what is next. It is important to plan for the nearest future. If you are asked where you will be in the next five years or ten years, you should be able to give a reasonable response. And beyond the plan, you must work towards that foreseeable future.

10

VISION PROVIDES DIRECTION

"Where there is no vision, the people perish: but he that keepeth the law, happy is he."
- **Proverbs 29:18, KJV**

Your direction, not your intentions, determines your destination. If you are traveling to a particular location and you take the opposite direction, even though your intention is a particular location, you can never make it there because you are on the wrong path. Your direction must never be disconnected from your intention. There must always be a path or a drawn-out plan on how to achieve your dream. It is exceptionally good to have a vision, but beyond the vision; it is more important to understand the path to fulfilling that vision.

As believers, we can seek God for direction. The Bible even says that we should not lean on our own understanding. As a result, we must learn to seek God and ask for a clear direction, before embarking on any journey in life and trust Him to lead till the end is in sight.

The Bible tells us of Peter's toiling in search of fish all night, but at the bidding and direction of Jesus, he was able to achieve a groundbreaking feat. His net broke and it took the assistance of the other ships nearby to get the fish to shore. This story points out the importance of following the direction of God. We cannot Go far if we lean on our understanding. We must ask for God's direction and walk the path.

Jesus is our perfect example on the visionary journey. There was a plan and there was a path to take in fulfilling that vision. At Jesus' birth, the angel told His earthly parents the purpose of His coming. He had a duty to fulfill and that was to save the world from destruction and to bring as many as possible to the Kingdom of God. Remember, Jesus is also God, but for this vision to be achieved, He had to come in the flesh. He had seen it and He knew that was the only way to saving mankind.

The big question we must constantly ask ourselves is the question of where? Where do you see yourself in the next five years or more? This question is a navigating factor on life's path. At different stages in life, you must answer the question of where. You cannot begin a journey until you know where you are going. You might not have the whole journey figured out, but it is important to have the end goal in mind. For instance, the goal of a medical student is to become a medical doctor after about six to seven years in the university. Once you have an end goal, you can always look past the seemingly obvious challenges and sail till the very end.

As Christians, our end goal is to make it to heaven, and that is at the close of this age. As a result, we are enjoined to focus on Christ, who is our role model and every obvious challenge can be easily surmounted. The Bible refers to Christ as the author and finisher of our faith. Understanding this should help us navigate the journey of life, fixing our gaze on him.

It is really saddening that most persons are just slumbering and gambling through life; they do not actually have a direction. When you begin something without a direction or plan in mind, you end up with nothing concrete to show for your effort.

Act on Your Dream

It is great to dream or have a clear vision, but it is important to be willing to act too. No matter how great a dream is, it will remain the realm of just dreams when it is not acted upon. In the words of Joel Brown, "*The only thing that stands between you and your dream is the will to try and the belief that it is actually possible."*

Willingness to act makes you able and helps you to persevere when challenges come your way. You must understand that no one will take up your dream any better than yourself. A story is told of a young man who dreamt of greatness. In his dream, he was very wealthy and he had people at his beck and call; he was greatly known far and wide. Suddenly, he woke up and realized it was all a dream. Instead of working towards being wealthy by putting in the extra work, he kept fantasizing and was waiting for the day he would wake up wealthy. He was not willing to pay the price of greatness and he died a pauper.

Vince Lombardi says, *"The difference between a successful person and others is not a lack of strength, not a lack of knowledge, but rather a lack of will."* No matter how beautiful an idea is, when it is not acted upon, it remains what it is, "an idea". When there is a drive, it comes with a willingness to pursue a set goal.

Facing difficulties would not be a problem when there is a drive to pursue a set goal. The story of Zacchaeus in the Bible rightly depicts the lifestyle of a person willing to surrender his all to Jesus. He wanted to see Jesus and to achieve this, he had to climb a tree. This act alone shows his willingness and readiness to let Jesus in. After Jesus came to his house, he willingly decided to make right his wrongdoings. In reality, it was not such an easy feat, but he was willing to renounce his old lifestyle and follow Jesus.

It is also important to remember that there is always a price to pay. Nothing exceptional comes easy. Your willingness to play your part helps to make the end goal clearer and even more achievable. The impossible becomes possible when you have a willing heart. A believer, who is heaven conscious, must be constantly willing to seek God's face and meditate on His word from time to time, so that growth can occur.

Willingness is a powerful tool that every idea thrives on because nothing can occur without it.

Understanding Times and Seasons

"Everything has seasons, and we have to be able to recognize when something's time has passed and be able to move into the next season," says Henry Cloud. Beyond visualizing your destination, it is essential that you understand the times and seasons. This is why you must be spiritually sensitive. As a Christian, understanding the seasons keeps you calm and hopeful that every vision will come to pass at its appointed time. The story of Abraham explains time and seasons clearly. God promised him that he would have a child. Several years passed and nothing happened. Sadly, it was within this period that Abraham slept with Sarah's maid and a child was born. I want to believe that both

Abraham and Sarah did not fully understand the timing and seasons of God. If they had, they would have patiently waited for the promised Isaac who eventually came.

When we lack the understanding of the seasons, there is a high probability that we will derail from the pathway to success, or rather find "quicker" (but destructive) means to achieve the set goal. It took the children of Israel forty years to get to the Promised Land. God understood that they needed to pass through a refining process before they could access the Promised Land. Unfortunately, so many of them perished in the wilderness because they lacked understanding of the seasons and they complained bitterly against the God who brought them out of Egypt.

1 Chronicles 12:32 tells of the sons of Issachar. We are told that they understood the times. They knew what Israel ought to do` and as a result, all their brethren were at their command. Like the children of Issachar, do you understand the times? This helps and greatly relieves you from unnecessary burdens. In life, there are seasons and they change. Even nature changes with seasons and time. We have the winter, spring, autumn, and summer, and each of these seasons comes with its peculiarities. Understanding helps you to navigate through the different seasons.

In life, there are good and bad seasons; understanding the peculiarity of the different seasons of life makes it easy to plan and overcome each. Also, understanding that tough times never last helps you to face each challenge squarely and come out stronger. It is important that you learn the lessons each season brings. The lesson shapes you and also drives you toward your foreseeable future.

Beyond understanding the times is knowing what you want because even if the season comes and you are clueless, it will swiftly pass by and the blessing and lessons will also pass with it. Remember, seasons come and go; they do not stay forever. Elisha, in 2 Kings 2:9-10, understood the times and made the best of it. Elijah, his boss, was soon to be taken away by God and Elisha was given a blank check. He could have missed the opportunity of a double portion, but he understood that his master was about to be taken away. While he was persevering and observant enough, the other sons of the prophets mocked him. Despite that, his stance was unwavering and he was focused. As a result, he did not miss that opportunity; he caught Elijah's mantle and the anointing of the double portion became his. May we have opened eyes to see and understand the times of life.

The gifts of God are precious to Him. For God to release His gifts to you, He wants to be sure that you can handle them. So, the question is, are you capable or ready to handle God's gifts? Elijah asked Elisha if he was truly ready for the double portion and from the scripture we can see that he was truly ready. He did not miss the chance. Elijah told Elisha he would have his request if he saw him depart and he did. He got the double portion; he desired it and it became his reality. Same with blind Bartimaeus - when others were trying to stop him from having what he saw, he cried louder. He knew Jesus was the answer to his problem and he pushed further. He understood the time and he did not let the moment slip away from him.

Dear reader, if you can see it, you can have it. God is willing to raise champions in this age, people of substance, people that He would take from the dunghill and place on the throne. But there is a prerequisite - they have to be people of understanding; knowing the times and seasons, and also knowing what to do. People who are not self-sufficient, but lean on God and seek Him for wisdom, understanding, and the ability to see. That is what makes the difference in a true believer.

11

THE MENTALITY OF KINGS

"Nothing can stop the man with the right mental attitude from achieving his goal; nothing on earth can help the man with the wrong mental attitude."
—**Thomas Jefferson**

I am excited that you have read to this point. It tells me that you are making good progress on your journey from the dunghill to the throne. Just to remind you, it is the desire of God that you get to the throne and remain there. He has promised that "the Lord will make you the head and not the tail; you shall be above only, and not be beneath..." (Deuteronomy 28:13).

However, for you to brave all obstacles and eventually get to the throne, you must have a king's mentality. You cannot think like a servant and hope to become a king. You cannot live and behave like a slave and hope that somehow you will get to the throne. The throne is meant for kings, and to sit on one, you have to think like a king.

Having the mentality of a king is not a walk in the park. If it were that easy to achieve, the word "mediocrity" would not have found a place in the dictionary. Toeing the path of mediocrity is the easiest thing to do because it takes nothing from you than to put your life on a steep road and leave it to run along like a car without brakes. The end will be disastrous of course, but it requires no effort from you other than to sleep and wake without a purpose, dream, or drive.

The scripture tells us that men are products of their thoughts; in other words, living like a king on earth has a lot to do with our mindsets and beliefs as individuals. A belief is defined as an opinion or a conviction that certain facts are true or exist. If you do not believe that God has made you a king and priest on earth, how will you even think or act like one?

Box of Limitations

There are some people who believe they cannot achieve certain feats or attain certain heights in life because no one in their family has ever done so. They believe they cannot own a car or a house because nobody in their family has ever owned such. These people have already put themselves in a box of limitations, from which they do not believe they can break free. People who reason like this have simply handed over the reins of their lives to fate and luck; they do not even try to be intentional about making their lives different from the pack.

Some families believe that they cannot rise above a certain level. I have also seen families that believe that since their forebears lived on welfare, it has to be so for them and their generations yet unborn. And because of this limiting mindset or mentality, it does not matter how much potentials, prospects, or qualifications they have, they will still go back to the pit because that is where they think they belong.

I am not saying any of this to condemn anyone; rather, I want you to know that we are principally products of our thoughts and imaginations. I want you to know that if you must reign like a king, you must begin to think like a king. Most importantly, I want you to know that it is in your DNA, as a child of God, to be a king on earth. I do not want you to remain in a lowly place when you can be all that God wants you to be.

I personally believe that our God is a God of excellence. When he created all of humanity, he looked down and saw that all He made was beautiful. This means that He is a God of brilliance and our lives are meant to carry the light which authenticates our heritage in Christ. I want to challenge you to break forth and desire to move to the next level. I do not want you to give up; I want you to know that the fact that you are reading this is proof that you are alive and because of that life, you have hope.

The Power in Your Mentality

To properly illustrate the power that lies in your mentality, I will be delving deeper into the story of the spies Moses sent to survey the land of Canaan, which I briefly mentioned earlier. I know you are probably familiar with the story already, but I want to implore you to stay with me as I unlock some additional truths I have discovered in the narrative.

In Numbers 13, God had spoken to the children of Israel through Moses that He was going to give them the land of Canaan. This is a factual statement of God already, concerning His plans for them. The whole idea was already finished in God's worktable and all He asked Moses to do was to select a few men to go on a tour of the dreamland. God did not send them there to seek their opinion on whether He should give them the land or not; He had already given it to them.

In my opinion, their trip was meant to be fun filled, more like an excursion in modern-day terms. But then, when the twelve spies came back with their reports, ten of them painted a grim picture:

> "But the men who had gone up with him said, "We are not able to go up against the people, for they are stronger than we. And they gave the children of Israel a bad report of the land which they had spied out, saying, "The land through which we have gone as spies is a land that devours its inhabitants, and all the people whom we saw in it are men of great stature. There we saw the giants (the descendants of Anak came from the giants); and we were like grasshoppers in our own sight, and so we were in their sight" (Numbers 13:31-33).

It was an evil report that broke the heart of the Israelites in the wilderness. We need to learn a very salient lesson from the ten spies who brought the bad news. The popular saying, "majority carries the vote" may not be right all the time. If we are to go by votes, we would have said that ten witnesses were enough to establish the truth. This is to let you know that spiritual matters cannot be interpreted from a carnal perspective. The majority does not always carry the vote when it comes to the dealings of God with humans. So, it is better to be with God, than to be with the majority that is not of God.

The ten spies were able to produce six negative statements from that single trip. A lot of Christians are like these men. All they see in every situation and circumstance is negativity. Even when God gives them loads and loads of precious promises, their lenses have been wired to only see impossibilities. While Caleb and Joshua were super excited and motivated to take over the land, the other ten had watered down the faith of others. They no longer believed the report of the Lord but those of the spies. Join me in this beautiful ride as we examine some of their claims.

One, "*We are not able to go up against the people, for they are stronger than us.*" It is like somebody saying, "This subject that I am doing in school is so tough, I can't even try it," "Oh, this examination you know, I can't even try it because it's so difficult." What is that opportunity you are ignoring in your life right now because you think that other people are better than you? Why will you even think that you are a non-entity when God affirms that you are created in His own image? That is not the mind of God for you. As long as the Lord is with you, you will conquer!

Two, "*The land through which we have gone as spies is a land that devours its inhabitants.*" This is the most amusing of their unfounded theories and I wish I could ask them a few questions in real life. "If the land is truly devouring its inhabitants, how come you still found people there that are alive and are living in that land? How come you went to the land that devours the inhabitants and you still came back alive?

This is a lesson for you and me to internalize. If anyone tells you something that does not sound right, it is better you go back to God for clarification. After all, he has assured us that He will guide us into all truth.

Three, "*There are giants in the land and we looked like grasshoppers.*" It seems as if the ten spies were trying so hard to convince the children of Israel about the danger of possessing the land that God had given them. If they looked like grasshoppers, how come the giants did not crush them with their large foot? How can the elect of God compare themselves to grasshoppers? Grasshoppers are insects with no spine or stamina, and when compared to giants, they amplified their belief that the possibility of having victory is zero.

Let me emphasize here that the words they spoke were the product of the mentality they had about Canaan after their espionage. Having the mentality of a pauper, a failure, or a mediocre is very deadly and has grave consequences. That is why you need to guard the door of your heart and mind. Be like the security operative that interrogates a stranger that pulls up in front of a king's home. Filter what you allow into your heart and mind; do not make your mind a fertile ground for a dunghill.

That the Scripture says what we speak reflects what is in our heart (Matthew 12:34) proves that mentality can make or mar an individual. Death and life are indeed in our thoughts. Therefore, the one who thinks evil, gets evil; while the one who thinks goodness, enjoys the goodness of God.

I feel so sorry for the ten doubting spies and all the people that they drew into unbelief. This, again, is why you need to be incredibly careful about the people who wield influence over your life because their negative mentality or energy can be easily transferred to you and the consequences could be severe.

Caleb and Joshua were the only ones who believed that they were able to go up and take over the land as God promised. The evil report that the other men brought caused the people to cry. It did not only make them cry, but it also made them sin against God by their murmuring and blasphemy. They forgot all about God's miracles in the past and said it would have been better for God to leave them in Egypt instead of promising them a better life that was non-existent. They uttered destructive words in the process and according to their thoughts and professions, they died in the wilderness and could not see that Promised land, with the exception of Joshua and Caleb.

You need to decide today who you will believe - God or society? God or the negative medical reports? God or the "experts" and seers, who are predicting gloom and doom? One thing is certain: You can hardly rise above your beliefs. It is not enough to desire good things. In fact, it is not enough for God to promise us good things in life; a lot of things are dependent on us, our words, and our thoughts. God cannot make His will done in our lives without our cooperation. He has given us the privilege of exercising our freedom and will never force us to do a thing. However, following and believing in God's promises for our lives is to our advantage.

The Mentality of the King of Kings

It is important for you to know God's thoughts about you, so that you will begin to align your thoughts with that of the King of Kings. God clearly says in Deuteronomy 28:13 that you will be the head and not the tail. In Isaiah 1:19, He says, you will eat the good of the land. This means that you can have the best car, make the best grades, live in the best house, and have a great job because that is God's desire for you.

In Jeremiah 29:13, God says that the thoughts He has for you are thoughts of peace, and not of evil, to give you an expected end. Why should you ever think or believe that the challenges you are facing right now will drown you when God has assured you that you will have a good end? It is the devil that wants to steal from you, kill you, and deprive you of joy, not God. And you must resist him, as a king resists a rebel or usurper.

You need a great deal of intentionality to know, believe, and also confess God's great promises for you. If God did not want the best for you, He would not make those beautiful promises concerning you. He does not lie and can never lie and you need to believe that His words are true.

12

REIGNING LIKE ROYALTY

"...His divine power has given to us all things that pertain to life and godliness, through the knowledge of Him who called us by glory and virtue"
- 2 Peter 1:3

Nothing good happens by chance or mere wishes. Knowing and understanding God's grand desires for you is one thing, doing your part to make it a reality is another. Sadly, a lot of people live their lives based on the "whatever will be will be" maxim. They forget that a person that God has purposed to be a medical doctor in life will never be one if he or she decides to drop out of med school "because it's too stressful".

If you are going to have the mentality of royalty and enjoy a royal lifestyle, you should understand that, as a royal personage, you cannot do what everyone is doing; you stand for what is true, even if the world is against you. You prepare conscientiously for the future and you are not ashamed to walk into the room of opportunities.

Some people are like the weather, they live like kings and queens when all is rosy, and activate the mediocre button when there are challenges. However, all we have considered so far is to help you develop and maintain the mindset of royalty throughout your lifetime. How can this be achieved?

The first thing you need to have on this journey is confidence. One of the key attributes of royals is confidence. I have never seen a king or queen with a poor self-image. Royals know who they are and what they carry. You too should know that you have a Father who owns the heaven and the earth and that being an heir to God means that you have unlimited access to the best of resources. You may ask yourself, *Who am I to be brilliant, gorgeous, talented, and fabulous?* Actually, who are you not to be? Your first major step to greatness is to believe in yourself and God's perception of you.

The second thing you need to have in order to live steadily like the royalty that you are is courage. I love Nelson Mandela's thoughts on courage, "*I learned that courage is not the absence of fear, but the triumph over it. The brave man is not the one who does not feel afraid, but he who conquers that fear*". I will not pretend to you that pursuing your dreams of living in dominion and fulfilling your destiny will not be fraught with difficulties and challenges. Nevertheless, it is in staying strong through the storms that you will be triumphant and have your dreams become your lifestyle. Always see challenges as unavoidable springboards for you to move to the next level.

Taking responsibility for your life is one of the fastest routes to making your lofty dreams a reality. It is a common saying that "*when a man points a finger at someone else, he should remember that four of his fingers are pointing at himself*". It sounds funny but, realistically, it is always much easier to blame others for your misfortunes and predicaments. It is easier to blame your parents for your failures than it is for you to rise and rewrite your story with your hands. It is easier to blame the economic situation of your country for your poverty than it is for you to rise and look for problems to solve in your community.

Enough of the blame game. As George Bernard Shaw rightly says, "*People are always blaming their circumstances for what they are. I do not believe in circumstances. The people who get on in this world are the people who get up and look for the circumstances they want, and if they cannot find them, make them.*" Living a royal life is your birthright; go for it and do not stop aiming for the skies!

You Are Not Alone

As you make up your mind to begin your journey from the dunghill to the throne, I want to assure you that you are not alone on your journey. God has promised to be with you. He has promised to walk with you, strengthen you and help you. This promise of God's presence and help as you walk your path should encourage and inspire faith in you Isaiah 43:1-2 says,

> *"But now, thus says the Lord, who created you, O Jacob, And He who formed you, O Israel: "Fear not, for I have redeemed you; I have called you by your name; You are Mine. When you pass through the waters, I will be with you; And through the rivers, they shall not overflow you. When you walk through the fire, you shall not be burned, Nor shall the flame scorch you."*

Are these not excellent words from the Almighty? These are reassuring words to you! Read the verses again until you feel the blessedness in the words. It does not matter what you go through on your way to the throne; it does not matter what life throws at you - you may pass through rivers, walk through fire, or even be surrounded by enemies - yet God will be with you! Imagine if you had to walk down a street with the president of the United States! How would you walk? Would you be afraid of anything or anyone? Absolutely not! Why should you, when you are walking with the most powerful person in the world? But

God is greater than any President in the world, and He has promised to walk with you on your journey.

Moreover, beyond just being with you, God says He will help you: *"Fear not, for I am with you; Be not dismayed, for I am your God. I will strengthen you, Yes, I will help you, I will uphold you with My righteous right hand"* (Isaiah 41:10). He will help you, regardless of what comes your way. Need I remind you that He is always faithful? He will keep His word to you and fulfill it to the letter.

In Genesis 28, we have the example of Jacob. When He left his parents to go to his uncle's place, he was unsure of what to expect; he couldn't even visualize what the future held for him. Before this time, he had supplanted his twin brother Esau and had stolen his blessing. As a result, Esau had threatened to kill him. So, when Jacob left his parents and his country to an unknown place, he began an untried journey with an uncertain fate and the threat of assassination by his brother hanging over his head.

But in Genesis 28, Jacob had an encounter with God that changed the dynamics of his journey in his favor. God promised him, *"Behold, I am with you and will keep you wherever you go, and will bring you back to this land; for I will not leave you until I have done what I have spoken to you"* (Genesis 28:15). God kept His promise of protection to Jacob and made his mission a success. Rest assured, therefore, that God's promises for you will come to pass.

Be encouraged, dear reader, and pursue God's plan for your life with the assurance of His presence and help. Be no longer dismayed or afraid; He who is with you is greater than whatever and whoever you may face on your way to the throne. If God be for you, who can be against you? Now that He is for you, can anything or anyone be against you? Can anything stop you from reaching the throne He has prepared for you? No! Never! Go in His might, therefore, and confront every challenge with the assurance of victory. You are a child of the King of kings and you have been redeemed to reign!

REFERENCES

CHAPTER ONE

Southerland, Mary (2015). "The Real Love Commandment". Retrieved from https://www.crosswalk.com/devotionals/girlfriends/the-real-love-commandment-girlfriends-in-god-february-17-2015.html

Roll, Yisroel (2017). "The Rejection of King David–Part One". Retrieved from https://torah.org/learning/torahtherapy-alone13/

CHAPTER TWO

Hill, Napoleon (2016). *Think and Grow Rich.* (Reprint). Napoleon Hill Foundation.

CHAPTER THREE

J. I. Packer (2000). "In God's Presence: Daily Devotions with J.I. Packer". Shaw

CHAPTER FOUR

Rensburg, Nick Van (2018). "Charge And Dominate Your Circumstances". Retrieved from http://www.amazinglovehawaii.com/wordfortoday/2016/6/16/time-to-take-charge-and-dominate-your-circumstances

CHAPTER FIVE

Lewis, C.S. (2002). *The Great Divorce.* HarperCollins

CHAPTER SIX

King, Martin Luther. "Why Jesus Called a Man a Fool," Sermon Delivered at Mount Pisgah Missionary Baptist Church on August 27, 1967.

Munroe, Myles (2015). *In Pursuit of Purpose.* Destiny Image; Second Edition.

CHAPTER SEVEN

William Jennings Bryan, Mary Baird Bryan (1900). "The Life and Speeches of Hon. Wm. Jennings Bryan"

Orlick, Terry (2015). *In Pursuit of Excellence 5th Edition.* Human Kinetics.

Rettig, Tim (2018). Struggling Forward: Embrace the Struggle. Achieve Your Dreams. Kindle edition

CHAPTER NINE

Swift, Jonathan (2019). *Vision is the Art of Seeing What is Invisible to Others.* Independently published.

CHAPTER TEN

Brown, Joel (Twitter post from Mar 09, 2017)

CHAPTER TWELVE

Shaw, G.B (1894). *Mrs Warren's Profession.* Floating Press.

www.ingramcontent.com/pod-product-compliance
Lightning Source LLC
Chambersburg PA
CBHW072040110526
44592CB00012B/1499